Orgasmic Leadership

Profiting from the Coming Surge in Women's Sexual Health and Wellness*

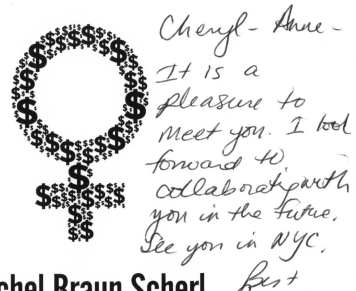

Cheryl-Anne—
It is a pleasure to meet you. I look forward to collaborating with you in the future. See you in NYC,
Best
Rachel

Rachel Braun Scherl

* EVERYTHING I KNOW I LEARNED AS A VAGIPRENEUR

INDIE BOOKS
INTERNATIONAL

Additional Copyrights and Trademark References
    Cialis® is a registered trademark of Eli Lilly and Company
    Fiera® is a registered trademark of AYTU Women's Health, LLC
    Levitra® is a registered trademark of Bayer Pharmaceuticals
    Orgasmic Leadership™ is a trademark of Amplify Growth, LLC
    Oscar® is a registered trademark of the Academy of Motion Picture Arts and Sciences
    Toms® is a registered trademark of Toms
    Tylenol® is a registered trademark of Johnson & Johnson, Inc.
    Sesame Street® is a registered trademark of Children's Television Workshop
    Vagipreneur® is a registered service mark of Amplify Growth, LLC
    Veru® is a registered trademark of Veru Inc.
    Viagra® is a registered trademark of Pfizer, Inc.
    vSculpt® is a registered trademark of Joylux, Inc.
    Zestra® is a registered trademark of Innovus Pharmaceuticals, Inc.

ISBN-10: 1-947480-15-4
ISBN-13: 978-1-947480-15-5
Library of Congress Control Number: 2018942595

Designed by Joni McPherson, mcphersongraphics.com

INDIE BOOKS INTERNATIONAL, LLC
2424 VISTA WAY, SUITE 316
OCEANSIDE, CA 92054
www.indiebooksintl.com

Table of Contents

Praise for *Orgasmic Leadership*

"Orgasmic Leadership *is a wonderfully insightful and incredibly relatable read on so many levels for the professional woman, working mom multitasker, looking for entrepreneurial knowledge, know-how and optimism to lean in to the women's health and wellness business."*

Dr. Alyssa Dweck, award winning gynecologist, voted "Top Doctor" in *New York Magazine* and in Westchester County, co-author of 3 books: *The Complete A to Z for your V, The Sexual Spark*, and *V is for Vagina*

"A market-maker in the multi-billion-dollar global women's sexual health marketplace, Rachel Braun Scherl is serious about smashing stereotypes and revealing inequities. Her super power is her passion, persistence, and perseverance on behalf of this huge, yet undervalued business opportunity."

Amy Millman, Co-Founder and President, Springboard Enterprises

"I am very impressed with Rachel's domain expertise, marketing chops and leadership. I've referred her to CEOs who could benefit from her wisdom, lessons learned and new vocabulary for FemTech. This book is essential reading for any "vagipreneur" and useful for all female entrepreneurs. Rachel tackles taboo topics with a delightful sense of humor. I'm sure you'll laugh out loud at times like I did."

Lauren Flanagan, Managing Partner, BELLE Capital USA; Partner, BiteSize Solutions

"Orgasmic Leadership *is a unique resource for women's sexual health and wellness—the first of its kind addressing all those silent concerns now out in the open."*

Marsha Firestone, Ph.D., President & Founder, Women Presidents' Organization

"With Orgasmic Leadership, *Rachel reminds us of two of my favorite topics, the power of female entrepreneurs and the importance of women's sexual health. Through her candid stories, probing interviews, and thought leadership she inspires us to think differently and never to give up our dreams for ourselves or our daughters."*

Lisa Kent, Founder, The Luminations Group and author of *Inspiring Innovation*

"Rachel Braun Scherl is a smart, fearless, female leader. She makes the complex, simple. Rachel can see a path forward, even when others may be having a hard time finding the way. This book is a must read for all women, who are seeking to be and do great in their careers."

Alissa Kaplan, Executive Director, J. Walter Thompson

*"*Orgasmic Leadership *is a game-changing read for women who want to get in the mix, make things happen and change the conversation."*

Lee Woodruff, author of the *New York Times* bestseller *In an Instant*

"Rachel is one of a kind, a real force of nature and has luckily turned her prodigious talents towards female health. As a vagipreneur and a person of action, Rachel is making things happen."

Kimberly Jenkins, Founder, Duke University Innovation and Entrepreneurship Initiative; Tech Executive (Microsoft, NeXT, Internet Policy Institute); Advocate, Mentor and Angel Investor for women-owned businesses

"What a great resource! Orgasmic Leadership *provides the vocabulary to have a powerful conversation about the important business of women's health. Rachel Braun Scherl's unique voice shares business insights with intelligence, humor and passion."*

Sue Hawkes, bestselling author of *Chasing Perfection*

"Rachel Braun Scherl is a creative and driven business person. Her success in building women's health businesses is a testament to her extraordinary imagination and persistence. As a speaker to MBA students and as a member of our university's entrepreneurial community, she is frank and direct. She is a source of inspiration as well as actionable practical advice."

Jon Fjeld, Executive Director, Center for Entrepreneurship & Innovation, The Fuqua School of Business at Duke University

"This book will empower you to challenge the conventional norms and help join the vagipeneur crusade to help clear a path to sexual vitality and equality."

Michael Krychman, MD, Executive Director of the Southern California Center for Sexual Health and Associate Clinical Professor at University of California, Irvine

"I recommend Orgasmic Leadership *to every patient and listener of mine who wants better insight and options regarding their sexual and reproductive health options. Rachel speaks with a powerful voice about building businesses and creating sexual, personal and professional options. Each interview adds a new layer of practical understanding. A must read."*

Beatty Cohan, author of *For Better, For Worse Forever*, nationally recognized psychotherapist and sex therapist

"I meet leaders, both male and female, every day in the work I do. In Orgasmic Leadership, *Rachel brings to life the characteristics and necessary mindset that I believe people need to be successful. And Rachel lives those qualities in her work and her life."*

Lindsay Mask, Founder and Executive Director of Ladies America, a global network of professional women

"Orgasmic Leadership provides a brave, honest, and enjoyable account of women's experiences as entrepreneurs. Rachel demonstrates how one can rush headfirst into challenges, with passion and grace. If you want to learn about dynamic leadership, read this."

Deborah Perry Piscione, *New York Times* bestselling author of *Secrets of Silicon Valley*

"Orgasmic Leadership shares inspirational stories of personal empowerment and professional transformation which is a treasure for every woman. My heartfelt respect, admiration and appreciation for Rachel Braun Scherl and all her sister entrepreneurs and vagipreneurs. These smart savvy women are changing the way we think, feel, and behave. Yay!"

Jackie Zeman, Emmy nominated TV actress

"When I started out as a medical journalist almost four decades ago, talking about colon cancer, prostates and, oh my, "lady bits" was not considered appropriate for the evening news. How times have changed, except for the part about "lady bits." For some reason we still have hang-ups about women's sexual health, much to the detriment of women everywhere. Finally, Rachel Braun Scherl has the courage to bring her passion and knowledge to educate and destigmatize discussions around female health and wellness. On behalf of men who want their female friends, lovers and partners to be healthy all over, thank you!"

Dr. Max Gomez, Emmy award winning medical correspondent and senior health editor for CBS

Dedication

"This above all: to thine own self be true."

Polonius, Hamlet Act 1, Scene III

Dad, even now that you are gone, yours is the voice that I hear in my head—the one that I have always heard. It is the voice that has always tried to guide me how to live, how to love, how to care, how to be kind, how to do good, how to build relationships, how to cry (apparently with reckless abandon), and how to make people laugh. Every day, you are a strong presence in my life. I see pieces of you in your grandchildren every day.

Mom, thank you for teaching me never to give up, for always being my biggest, unwavering supporter. With your fervent desire to help solve problems, I learned how to forge a new path if the one in front of me was blocked. You taught me to believe in my value as a person, a mother, a sister, a family member, a professional—and in all of the other roles I play in my life. And you showed me how to celebrate joy and to laugh.

Being loved by you has made me feel brave, strong, and capable.

SECTION 1

Why Should Anybody Care about "Lady Business"?

CHAPTER 1

Why the Women's Sexual Health and Wellness Business Is Exploding

"It's supposed to be hard. If it wasn't hard, everyone would do it. The 'hard' is what makes it great."

—Tom Hanks as Jimmy Dugan, *A League of Their Own*

Would it shock you to know that I didn't start my business career intending to become a "vaginal" crusader? When I was a child, I thought I might be a firefighter, a ballerina, an Olympic gymnast, or a figure skater, to name just a few options. I did not anticipate that after twenty-plus years as a marketer of pharmaceutical, consumer health, beauty, and wellness products, I would be in the *vagina* business, assuming a role, somewhat accidentally, as a warrior for women.

Today I speak to business leaders about the trials, tribulations, travesties, and triumphs I have experienced as a female executive fighting to bring awareness and easy access to women for products and services designed to meet a range of needs. I work directly with these companies to help them find creative ways to build these businesses.

That is my job. I am a Vagipreneur.

Wait. *What did I just say?*

Yes, I said Vagipreneur—a moniker I hold dear (thank you to the great journalist and creator of this unique job, Abby Ellin), which succinctly describes a person in the business of female sexual health and wellness. And today I say it boldly, without whispering, out in the open, loudly, where (gasp) *children* might hear me.

Well, not *purposely* near the children, but it happens from time to time.

That's by design. Because the biggest business challenge in female health is the one against uncomfortable silence; the discomfort with the conversation and, specifically, the lack of appropriate language to describe female sexuality in all its complex glory. I learned early on in this Vagipreneurial journey that once I made that proclamation and declared my role in this societal battle, it got (and remains) downright crazy—every man (and in my case, woman) for herself.

Until my daughter was twelve years old and my son was nine (they are now twenty-two and nineteen—yikes), I worked on businesses and products that frankly, didn't interest them. They knew Mommy was a consultant (whatever that meant). They knew Mommy's work took her to boring places that did not interest them, like Columbus, Houston, Denver, or Raleigh, as well as exciting places they could not picture, like Budapest, China, and Brazil.

Well, all of that benign disinterest on their part (and on the parts of lots of other people who seemed to nod off when they asked me what I did—*you know who you are*) changed when I became a Vagipreneur, cofounding and running a business that had a pioneering product to improve arousal, desire, and satisfaction for women of all ages and at all life stages.

Suddenly, Mommy's work became the subject of every conversation with anyone, anywhere, at any time, and not necessarily in a time or place of my choosing—or theirs. Overnight, after years of a fair level of social disinterest in my career (a symptom that I had first noticed when I moved to the suburbs), I became extremely popular at dinner parties and girls' nights out. Despite my repeated comments that I was in the business of female health and not the delivery of care, women asked me questions as if I were a younger Dr. Ruth.

Now, at heart, I am a storyteller and salesperson. I am always up for engaging in, starting, and creating conversations that provide the important information that will lead to a sale. But I discovered there are literally unimaginable places, times, and contexts in which a Vagipreneur might hear about intimacy challenges. It seemed wherever I went and whatever I did, family members, friends, strangers, and even proverbial butchers, bakers, and candlestick makers were stalking me to ask questions. Very personal questions. *Seriously* personal questions. The questions were not only about the products I was working on, but more often than not, about each person's sexual challenges, victories, and knowledge gaps.

The questions were about everything and anything—relationships, positions, pains, waxing—nothing seemed to be out of bounds. *How does the product work? Why don't I have vaginal orgasms? How can I get in the mood when all I feel right now is fury because my husband doesn't help around the house?* (No product can fix that, as far as I know.) *Rachel, will this product help me stop thinking about my to-do list during sex?* (No kidding; we did research and women said that.) *You said this product is topical; does that mean I always have to be on top?* (No, I'm not even paraphrasing here.)

Did I mention (I know I did) that when I embarked on this chapter of my life, my kids were young and didn't necessarily need to hear that a grown-up with whom we carpooled had hurt her pelvis with an uncommon, inventive, and clearly dangerous *move*?

Some of the details and questions I heard about people's lives were so personal, in some states they may have been illegal—more on that later. In all fairness and seriousness, you can't be taken seriously in female health without having developed some expertise given its importance, tons of data, and scores of details about women's sexual lives and responses. I *did* have a lot of information at my fingertips—about female sexual health, about how products work, about what folks in the medical field say, about new offerings on the horizon, about the results of clinical studies, about the options. You name it, I could and can talk about it. But I certainly didn't want to give lectures about the complexities of female sexual response and the multiple physiological and psychological systems at play while sitting in a friend's living room, watching the Super Bowl, with *my* kids and *their* kids sitting there.

Boundaries, people.

Still, I couldn't escape the questions. Neither could my impressionable children. The information seekers were everywhere.

For my children, I have always tried to provide age-appropriate, clear descriptions of what I did to arm them with facts. As the daughter of a therapist, I was trained to be a big fan of openness. I thought I was incredibly modern and forward-thinking as I talked with my children about intimacy, appropriate clinical names for body parts, love, marriage, and intercourse. I admit I started with the old, "when two people love each other very much, and they are married…" speech. At some point, and not recently, they clearly figured out that people had sex outside of marriage. I told them that physical intimacy is an important part of a relationship and that, for a lot of reasons, sometimes women do not enjoy the experience as much as they want to. And that Mommy's company made a product that helps couples enjoy each other in that part of their relationship.

I was feeling quite proud of myself regarding the clarity and honesty of my parental communication—until my son said, "Oh I get what you do, Mommy. My autobiography could be called *Diary of a Pimpy Kid*."

Let me tell you, your parental confidence cannot help but take a precipitous nosedive when one of your children thinks you are a pimp. And by the way, *how did he even know what a pimp was?* Clearly, I should have done a better job of monitoring his screen time; I was sure that at any minute, a child protective agency would swoop in and say that my children were living in an inappropriate (maybe even unsafe) environment.

But lest you think *that* was the most embarrassing point in my Vagipreneurial life, I promise you, it was just one of many (oh so many).

There was also one particularly memorable instance when I was minding my own business, playing with my daughter in a park, when an acquaintance (and I really do mean *just* an acquaintance) came up to us and whispered, "Do you have your car here?"

"Sure," I answered. "Do you need a ride?"

"No," she said. "I heard you have *stuff* in your car."

OK, fabulous; now I was a pimp *and* a drug dealer. I could just feel the Mother-of-the-Year nominations rolling in.

And that was before the inevitable question from my daughter upon hearing this conversation. "Mommy, what do you have in your car?'

I admit it: I cracked under the pressure. "Hey," I said enthusiastically, "Let's go have ice cream and french fries for dinner while we watch TV. And maybe you can go to school late tomorrow." Listen: sometimes you need to throw a Hail Mary pass.

Regardless of what I did for a living, my kids, like most, didn't like it when I went on business trips. I remember their sweet little faces at the window, crying as I walked out with my black rolling bag, the international sign of child abandonment.

One day my Vagipreneurial work offered a bit of inspiration. I was staffing the phones, speaking to customers, as we required everyone in the company to do. During one call, a woman shared enthusiastically (OK, she was shouting), "This stuff really works. Thank you, God!" After that, when I had to go on business trips, I assured my children that I was out doing "God's work." Lesson: You use the tools you have at your disposal.

Both of my children switched schools the same year I bought the company. I would say these were unrelated events, but at their old schools, their friends knew about my job, and their friends' parents were my friends, so they *also* knew about my job. I imagine that I am the only mother around who jokes that her children voluntarily entered the *Vagipreneur Protection Program*.

I developed a much thicker skin as the months and years went by, as did my kids. But those early months opened my eyes to several things.

First, a lot of women were eager to get their hands on the product and to open up about challenges in the bedroom—sometimes inappropriately eager, considering the age and proximity of our young bystanders. I sometimes felt as if I were at an out-of-control concert, in danger of being stampeded by a herd of desperate women. Second, and somewhat paradoxically, women didn't immediately leap at the opportunity to try the product without a bit of education and exploration about how it worked to enhance the experience of female sexuality in all of its complexity. And finally, it became clear that in American society, we don't actually have a ready vocabulary to discuss these matters in ways that work for many women.

We have all been schooled in the language of male sexual dysfunction, thanks to inescapable advertising. But words like "bigger," "longer," and "stronger" do not generally reflect how women talk and feel. And when I say that, I am not just offering a personal opinion. In my work, I have spoken to literally hundreds of women about their feelings, concerns, anxieties, and joys about sex. They have told me, without hesitation, that they do not look at sex as a performance activity, and therefore, many of those adjectives simply do not apply.

How do you have a conversation without a common vocabulary? How do you create interest in a discussion and options when the words available quickly devolve into territory that is unrelatable at best and prurient, unsavory, and disrespectful at worst? I could hardly be upset about my son's use of the word "pimp" when that word might show up in some of the top-ranked Google matches for "female sexual arousal" or "women's sexual enjoyment." The truth of the matter is, there is an exceedingly fine line between legitimate sexual health and wellness products and the other side of that proverbial line. Just look at cultural references we hear all the time. The Tony Award-winning best musical, *Avenue Q*, a play for grown-ups populated with Sesame-Street-like puppets, acknowledges "The Internet is for Porn" in an entire song of the same title (in which one of the puppets also sings, "Grab your dick and double-click")—and while one might question the combination of puppets and porn, the show has been touring the country to sold-out audiences since 2003.[1]

And don't get me started about a whole generation of young adults whose entire sexual education comes from watching online porn—a world of simultaneous orgasms and depictions of "erotic" violence. (On a serious note, *anything* is fair game between consenting adults.) Cindy Gallop, a dynamic advertising executive turned entrepreneur (whom I profile in this book), focuses on one of the most important questions in the conversation: *What happens when today's total access to hardcore porn converges with our society's equal total reluctance to talk openly and honestly about sex?* Her answer was to create MakeLoveNotPorn.tv, a site for user-generated content that bills itself as *Pro Sex. Pro Porn. Pro Knowing the Difference.*[2]

What's Good for the Gander Is...Banned for the Goose?

You've seen the ads. You've heard them. On TV. In print. On the radio. Online. Everywhere. Anywhere. You can't escape them. They come at you from all directions, in every possible medium.

By now, is there anybody alive in America who doesn't know there's a "little blue pill" for men that treats erectile dysfunction, or about the "four-hour erection?" Since its arrival on the market in 1998, few prescription drugs have entered the popular consciousness like Viagra. The sexual dysfunction medication was endorsed by the likes of former presidential candidate Bob Dole and international soccer star Pelé, and while these names may not carry much weight with millennials or Generation Z, they helped to usher the drug and the conversation about men's sexual satisfaction into the mainstream.

---

[1] https://www.allmusicals.com/lyrics/avenueq/theinternetisforporn.htm.

[2] https://talkabout.makelovenotporn.tv.

Viagra ads, and ads for its fellow erectile dysfunction drugs, penetrated our consciousness so deeply and thoroughly that late-night comedians can still riff on "erections lasting four hours" and *everybody* knows exactly what ads—and which products—are being discussed, even if they aren't specifically named. Eventually, other erectile dysfunction pharmaceuticals, like Cialis and Levitra, took their place beside "The Big V."

Cialis created instantly iconic print ads with consenting adults sitting side-by-side in matching his-and-hers bathtubs in a green, grassy meadow—as do we all, from time to time, don't we? (Seriously, *what is with those bathtubs*? Philosophically, I think I get it; the tubs are symbols of relaxing, taking your time, not hurrying. Sure, a bath is more relaxing and indulgent than a quick shower. And I believe that the Cialis advertising team was trying to create a warmer, gentler, more inviting positioning for their product than ads for Viagra—more feminine, as it were. However, in all my years on this planet, I have yet to see or hear of a couple dragging clawfoot bathtubs to the beach, getting in them, and watching the sunset.)

When I speak to people about this category, I often start with a query to demonstrate the chasm that exists between male and female vocabularies around this topic. I ask, "Who is looking for a partner with a four-hour erection? Raise your hands high." As you might expect, I generally don't see too many hands go up. And I have yet to find the woman who emphatically says, "Me! *That* is what I am looking for!"

But money talks and business is business. The global erectile dysfunction market is expected to reach nearly $4.25 billion by 2022, according to a 2016 study by Research and Markets, so it's no surprise that marketers and advertisers are eager to get the word out about products they've developed to help the men suffering from the problem.[3] Globally, the advertising spend for erectile dysfunction products exceeds $300 million annually. And by the way, estimates suggest that as many as 50 percent of users take the product for performance *enhancement,* as opposed to treatment for actual sexual dysfunction (not that there is anything wrong with that).

And yet.

Men are objectively *not* the only people who suffer from sexual arousal, concerns, difficulties, and disorders. Not by a long shot.

In 2008, my longtime and adored business partner, Mary Wallace Jaensch, and I created Semprae Laboratories, Inc. with a venture capital partner. Given Mary's incredible background and experience before me (Mt. Holyoke, Yale School of Management, and Procter & Gamble, to name a few) as well as with me, we just assumed that we had the combined grit, skill, and passion to build this company. And so forward march we went. We built the company by women, for women (*funded* by women partners at venture capital firms), focusing on marketing Zestra Essential Arousal Oils—a safe, nonhormonal, topical product targeted at women's sexual arousal and satisfaction. We believed we'd hit the motherlode. In America alone, an estimated 43 percent of women (30 million at that time) reported some form of female sexual dysfunction (FSD), which is clinically defined as persistent and recurrent problems with sexual response, desire, orgasm, or pain that distresses the woman or causes strain in her relationship with her partner.[4]

---

[3] Research and Markets. "Erectile Dysfunction Market - Global Outlook and Forecast 2018-2023." *Research and Markets - Market Research Reports - Welcome,* 13 Feb. 2018, www.researchandmarkets.com/research/kwz4rc/global_erectile?w=4.

[4] Laumann, Edward O., A. Paik, and RC Rosen. "Sexual Dysfunction in the United States: Prevalence and Predictors." JAMA. February 10, 1999. https://jamanetwork.com/journals/jama/fullarticle/188762.

Zestra had already been clinically tested in a placebo-controlled, double-blind study for safety and efficacy. That's a pharmaceutical study model, even though Zestra was classified as a cosmetic rather than a drug. The study had found Zestra increased arousal, feelings of arousal, desire, feelings of desire, and satisfaction for women of all ages and life stages. The clinical evidence indicated that it worked for seven out of ten women (I might also add, we heard from customers that it was "life-changing" for about four in ten). Formulated from a patented blend of botanical oils and extracts that increased the sensitivity of nerve endings to increase deep, pleasurable sensations, Zestra seemed positioned to explode in the marketplace.

What could possibly go wrong? We had a plan, funding, relevant experience, drive, and an amazing product. Zestra was a topically applied product, with no known drug/drug interactions, used on demand, and it didn't lose effectiveness after repeated usage. The product included no parabens, glycerin, or hormones. And there was no other product on the market that performed the same way and could make such significant claims about such an important topic.

Once we refined the packaging, product, and marketing message (the stuff we had spent our careers doing), we were off to the races. We believed in the product, and we thought all it would take to succeed would be getting the word out. It worked for Viagra and the like: why not Zestra? *Sounds easy,* right?

Based on our decades of experience marketing pharmaceuticals and health and wellness products and building a successful business as partners, not to mention tons of Zestra-specific market research including nineteen sets of focus groups, two statistically projectable quantitative studies which included hundreds and hundreds of women, and the overwhelming response of friends and acquaintances, we knew we had something special on our hands. The existing market for women's lubricants alone was $200 million, and this product had the opportunity to do so much more.

Much to our amazement, it wasn't long before we felt like Tom Hanks as Jim Lovell in *Apollo 13:* "Houston, we have a problem."

CHAPTER 2

My Journey as a Vagipreneur

I t was 2008, and the bottom was falling out of the financial markets. Mary and I found ourselves in Silicon Valley—two women, one in her forties, the other in her fifties—talking to venture capital firms about vaginas.

We had run businesses and consulted for businesses, but we had never raised money; certainly not serious, venture-capital amounts of money. I was the type who didn't like calling other parents at my children's school for $0.25 for a bake sale, but apparently, I was comfortable asking people for millions of dollars to grow a "vagina business."

We had booked thirteen appointments with venture capital firms in two days. At that pace, even though each firm communicates what it believes is a different strategy, expertise, and market focus, these kinds of meetings become a blur to the entrepreneur—an indistinguishable parade of offices, from the lovely receptionist who greets you at the front desk right down to the file cabinets, dress code, male/female ratio (disheartening) and investment criteria (often indistinct, despite what they usually describe as very specific investment theses).

We went into the first meeting and right off the bat, we encountered the most obvious question: How was our product different from Viagra?

Great question. Seriously.

We had the answer all lined up, and we laid it out in scientific detail. Viagra, we explained, works as a vasodilator (it opens blood vessels), which increases blood flow, and male genitalia work like a hydraulic pump, so increased blood flow means the pump "gets pumped up," leaving men basically ready to go. On the other hand, increased blood flow is only *one part* of what is necessary for a woman's sexual response and enjoyment. And on we went sharing the knowledge that was relevant to the question.

As we continued to provide a detailed explanation of how the female sexual response was different and more complex, we could hear the snickers, see eyes glazing over or, in some cases, rolling back up into heads (which, by the way, is a far more disconcerting response than the constant checking of phones or childish laughter).

Meeting one: A pitch and a strike. Needless to say, we didn't get funding at that meeting or a request for follow-up (a necessary sign to move towards a financing)—*nothing*.

At the second meeting, the men in the room (again, mostly white, mostly in their thirties and forties) had a different question, which was unsurprising. It was also one they apparently found totally amusing: "What does it do for *him?*"

Undaunted, we described the intended use of the product—*for women*—and clarified that the results of the clinical studies focused on *her* arousal, desire, and feelings of satisfaction. Anecdotally, we shared that *his* increased satisfaction with the product was likely the result of enjoying the satisfaction of his partner, or feeling more confident and competent as a partner (all of the studies were done with heterosexual couples in long-term relationships).

Apparently, a woman's increased satisfaction was not interesting enough to this group, and at the end of that meeting, we again saw no sign of the follow-up meeting that would indicate any hope of obtaining funding. And we may have allowed ourselves just one minute to wonder aloud on our way to the next meeting whether anybody had *ever* asked what Viagra would do for *her* in the early stages of the little blue pill's product development.

Meeting two: Strike two—we didn't even get a piece of the ball. Now we were 0-for-2. We knew we needed to adjust our game (and our swing) drastically.

Now, a brief aside: I am by nature a credit-card-only person. I like to track all my expenditures (not that I ever look back at them). In case of emergency or personal request, I can tell you exactly what I spent on groceries in June 1994. I rarely carry cash. But on that day in 2008, in the midst of the global economic downturn, with companies like Shearson Lehman going bankrupt, for some reason, either through some sort of divine intervention or dumb luck, I just happened to have a $100 bill in my wallet. And that $100 bill was both our inspiration and our pitch meeting savior.

Mary and I huddled after the second meeting and decided to go for it in the next meeting (number three out of thirteen for those counting at home)—really try to shake things up and approach the conversation differently in the hopes of getting to a substantive discussion about funding. I mean, eleven more meetings like the first two seemed more like a prison sentence than a great business opportunity.

As we walked into the next pitch meeting, I pulled the $100 bill, as planned, out of my wallet and slammed it onto the table with a resounding *thwack,* then paused for dramatic effect. I made my opening statement. "Here is a hundred-dollar bill. If anybody here makes a double *entendre* or joke that we haven't heard before, shares a sexual innuendo that makes us uncomfortable, asks a question about the category that we cannot answer, or even makes us blush, this hundred-dollar bill is yours."

I paused again—a pregnant pause (pun intended). And then delivered what we intended to be a knock-out—the real opening salvo. "She likes it more. She wants to have it more. Now let's talk about the business model."

Total and complete silence.

Now we finally had their attention.

At that moment, the energy in the room completely changed. With that opening, we had communicated that we could take anything thrown at us. That we knew business—and *our* business. That we weren't amateurs. That we couldn't and wouldn't be embarrassed. That we were business people talking about a business opportunity, not people looking to laugh about sex with a bunch of strangers. That we were serious about bringing this product to a wider market. So if anybody in the room sitting around the table needed to get anything out of their systems, they could feel free to make seventh-grade locker room jokes (no offense intended to most seventh-graders, who generally exhibit a higher level of maturity than what we saw in some of our pitch meetings). And finally, that after they got their giggles out and finished the side glances and frat-house backslapping, we'd still be standing in front of them, ready to talk about Zestra.

Ultimately, over the next four years, the dynamic created by that $100 bill changed the way we talked about the product and the business. We were frank and engaged in important discussions about women's sexuality (discussions which continue to be a driver of my work today). And yes, we were going to talk about vaginas.

And clitorises. And labia. And more. We were going to use all the anatomically correct words to talk about women's sexual pleasure and satisfaction. We were going to talk about orgasms, lubrication, and enhancement without apologizing, without compromising—and of course, without blushing.

Spoiler alert: We did ultimately successfully raise tens of millions of dollars for Zestra and got the product into more than 2,000 Walmarts, in addition to building a direct-to-consumer business.

And nobody *ever* got our $100 bill.

We Didn't Know What We Didn't Know

Over more than twenty years in business, Mary and I have contributed to building many businesses and brands. Many are household names; others are small companies that you have never heard of (yet). The common thread is that they fight hard to gain customers and generate business traction. It often takes creativity and out-of-the-box thinking, but with the right leadership, growth strategy, and sales and marketing plans, among other factors, ultimately, many businesses can and do grow.

So what does it take when the road to business growth is ever longer, bumpier, and filled with potholes that are sometimes big enough to swallow an entire vehicle?

As a business strategist, entrepreneur, and Vagipreneur, I have experienced firsthand the challenges that stand in the way of building businesses and the perseverance required to gain traction when people strive to accomplish things that go against the grain or require a change in behavior. These challenges face all businesses, but we had no reason to believe that any of challenges couldn't be overcome—or that what had worked for Viagra wouldn't work for Zestra.

I cut my teeth in marketing at Johnson & Johnson and met people who have been instrumental in my growth as a person and professional, working on brands you probably have in your home right now, including Tylenol. I earned an MBA from the Stanford Graduate School of Business. I worked as an employee for other consulting firms and started my own. I have worked on hundreds of projects for products and services affecting women, from the tops of their heads to the tips of their toes and every body part in between. You name it, and I've marketed a product for a woman's particular life stage or health need: haircare, skincare, menstruation, fertility, birth control, and cures for the oh-so-glamourous hemorrhoids and foot fungus. For more than a decade before my partner, Mary, and I decided to create our female sexual health company, we had built and run a successful consulting firm, finding creative ways to market and promote products in the health and wellness space. So we weren't naïve. We felt prepared when a friend in venture capital (who—big surprise—was not focused on or interested in this space) handed us information about Zestra and said, "I think you two could take this company somewhere. This is right up your alley."

Flash forward. After four months of complete immersion in the category and product while simultaneously running our consulting practice, we were taking the company somewhere.

What we didn't know when we started our journey with Zestra was that everything we experienced in that first couple of fundraising meetings would play out on a much larger canvas as we ran into obstacle after obstacle trying to educate our target market (and funders) about the product.

I certainly didn't know that media outlets would lock down as tight as a nuclear reactor in meltdown the moment they were faced with the subject of female sexual satisfaction. After all, why would I ever have suspected such a thing? ED ads were on the air night and day and had been for a decade at that point, or on major networks, during major sporting events like the Super Bowl. Why on earth would *Lifetime* not want us running our ads on their station at 8:30 p.m., when I am quite confident no young children were watching? And how could we possibly have imagined that we would be offering to spend significant money on ads (yes, pay them actual money— *large sums of money* for a new company) on other media channels and that they would say, "No thanks," time and time again?

As a part of a strategy to roll out the product to a broader market, Mary and I worked with professionals to create tasteful, factual, accurate, and effective ads for Zestra. There was nothing prurient or objectionable about them; we didn't simulate sexual activity, as did other companies advertising products completely unrelated to sex (sneakers and toilet bowl cleaners, among others). We didn't even use the names of female body parts (again, not that there is anything wrong with that). From our perspective, the ads were fairly innocuous and certainly respectful. One ad, for instance, simply said, "Try Zestra Essential Arousal Oils for Free." We aggressively contacted more than 100 media outlets to make what we thought would be straightforward media buys on networks— always a long shot—along with cable TV, radio, and websites. We had absolutely no reason to believe that buying advertising space would be anything other than routine. "You have ad space, we have money"—done, right?

And then *ninety-five percent of the media outlets we contacted* refused to take our money. Not even WebMD—a medical site— would ultimately agree to take our ads. Even though Zestra was a safe, clinically-proven product, it quickly became crystal clear that we would not, under any circumstances, be able to persuade the majority of advertisers to accept Zestra ads in the places, channels, and outlets where we knew our target customers would be watching, listening, or reading.

Thankfully, the seemingly endless chorus of people saying "No" wasn't the end of my story as a Vagipreneur; it was just the beginning.

Have you ever seen the movie *Network*, in which Peter Finch, playing Howard Beale, an exasperated news reporter, has a fit on camera? He declares, "I want all of you to get up out of your chairs. I want you to get up right now and go to the window. Open it, and stick your head out, and yell, *'I'm as mad as hell, and I'm not going to take this anymore!'*[5] I love that sentiment. It certainly described my feelings at the time. But you can't successfully sell female satisfaction if you are "mad as hell." You have to get the screaming out of your system, then get back to work—with a smile on your face.

I am still smiling, many years into what has become a passion project for me, which continues to grow, expand and motivate me: to build female health businesses (broadly defined as reproductive health, sexual health and wellness); to share the lessons I've learned along the way as well as the mistakes I have made; to learn from others who are bravely building companies in this space; and to encourage other Vagipreneurs to enter the void. There's a wide-open playground in the female sexual health and wellness marketplace, and it's growing and maturing every day. The excitement is there, the customers are there, and for sure, the money is there.

---

[5] *Network*. Directed by Sidney Lumet. United States: United Artists, 1976. Film.

No Time Outs...

Growing up, movie night at my house was not only for Disney princesses or heartwarming, soft-focus, family-friendly, G-rated fare. No; our entertainment coordinator was my dad, and he was a huge fan of come-from-behind, dig-deep, take-all-comers sports-training movies—think *Rocky* (I-V), *Rudy*, *Breaking Away*, and *Brian's Song*.

My favorite, by far, and the one that most informed our life view (and was a source of continued inspiration with Zestra), was a film that starred James Caan—the brutal 1975 cult action/horror classic, *Rollerball*.[6] Now, I am quite confident that this film is not appropriate family-bonding viewing for many families. But we were, and are, a competitive bunch.

In the film, the premise of Rollerball (the game) is simple and insane: men on roller skates, wearing spiked gloves, race around an inclined track, sometimes towed by other burly men on speeding motorcycles, engaging in a brutal, gladiatorial, deadly version of roller derby. Anything goes, including maiming or killing other players. Teams score by taking possession of and shooting goals with a solid, injury-inflicting silver ball. In fact, victory is not declared until the other team is entirely maimed or dead. (OK, I *said* it wasn't *The Sound of Music*). And before every match, the rules of engagement are declared: "No time outs; no substitutions."

Loosely translated?

There is no quitting—period. There is no one on the bench to take your place. People are counting on you. Your success and the success of those around you depends on your efforts. You have to be 100 percent in the game. You have to play hard, and even more importantly, you have to play until you can't play anymore.

---

[6] *Rollerball*. Directed by Norman Jewison. 1975. Film.

The same rules, it turns out, also apply to entrepreneurship, to business-building, and yes, to the business of female sexual health, because you are playing on a field where calling time-out (on fundraising, growing the business, finding customers) is the kiss of death.

Whether a female health business is helping alleviate pelvic pain, incontinence (which affects both men and women), feminine hygiene, or satisfaction, many entrepreneurs in the "lady business" space today have and will inevitably find themselves hitting unexpected barriers, running up against different standards than those that apply to other businesses.

But that's *never* a signal to take a time-out. That's the signal to dig in. And dig in we did, despite the pushback and ignorance, as every Vagipreneur profiled in this book does. There was certainly no time or place for a time-out.

During fundraising meetings for Semprae Laboratories, the parent company that produced Zestra, conversations stopped cold if men in the room were uncomfortable or not interested in discussing the product due to *their* perceived lack of a need for it. I cannot count the number of times I heard variants of, "This must not be a very common issue because my wife has never mentioned problems. I am not sure this product has big market potential."

Why? Because *you* are absolutely sure you are such a skilled lover, and she is totally satisfied? Or could it be, perhaps, because this is literally the *one* category (among the dozens and dozens I have worked on) that women in long-term committed relationships don't discuss—not with their friends, their moms, sisters, aunts, cousins, or partners?

My hypothesis is this: If you share with anybody the intimate details of your life, it is likely that you are friends with and socialize with that person. For instance, one day you might say to a friend, "My husband used to do this trick where he hung from a chandelier during sex, which I loved, but now he doesn't. I miss it. That kept things alive." And then the very next day, you might find yourself out to dinner with both your formerly acrobatic partner and your confidante—with his or her partner, too. And at that moment, the chandelier-swinging reveal feels *inappropriate*—as if you have violated some oath or tried to emasculate your partner in some way— neither of which would do much for your sex life, as a couple. So, no; it's highly unlikely that the partners of the men in the boardrooms with us had ever mentioned problems. *To the men.* That doesn't mean there were no problems.

Here's the thing: Erectile dysfunction is right there, out in the open, as it were. There's no hiding it, no pretending it doesn't exist or doesn't affect sexual experience, pleasure, enjoyment, willingness, or mood. And the fix, as we explained (probably in too much detail) in those meetings, is also relatively straightforward: If the pump isn't working, fix the pump. For women, sexual response is an integrated, complex web of physiological, psychological, emotional, contextual, and social reactions, cues, and responses. It is not "*all* in our heads," but some of it certainly is.

Women can (and do) often minimize, avoid, try to hide, make excuses, and otherwise look for ways *not* to come right out and say, "Something has changed." Or, "Honey, I am not enjoying this." Or, "It feels different." Or, "I am not really having an orgasm." Or, "This doesn't feel great, and sometimes it doesn't even feel *good.*" Or, "Occasionally it's just a mechanical chore. I wish it weren't the case, but it is." Or, "Sometimes I am making to-do lists in my head when we are having sex" (also validated by research).

The reasons women don't come right out and talk about their sexual concerns and difficulties are numerous and varied. For some women, care and consideration for their partners, lack of knowledge about their own body and its responses, or no positive experience to compare to may be the cause. For others, shame, trauma, cultural norms, family tradition, religion, social embarrassment, or lack of a vocabulary may prevent an open discussion of such issues—even with their personal physicians. Some women are raised to believe sex is for procreative purposes only and may not even understand or believe sex *can* be enjoyable. And many women are utterly unaware of the many common factors that can change or decrease their enjoyment and sexual experiences: side effects of oral contraceptives, the physical and emotional aftermath of cancer treatment, obesity, illness, many common medications, stress; the list goes on. (It has always struck me as particularly ironic that oral contraceptives can impact your desire. So now you can have sex without fear of pregnancy, but you don't want to? As Rita Rudner, the comedian, might say—and I am paraphrasing—"If there is a God, I think he is into practical jokes.")

In a nutshell, ladies, you are not doing anything wrong. And companies, many started by women, have only recently been developing the tool kit that offers women the language, the solutions, and the confidence to talk about it all.

Early in discussions with potential investors, we had two choices. We could continue to address common objections *ad nauseum* (a process that seemed doomed to take the rest of our natural lives): misperceptions like women's sexual satisfaction isn't a big deal, and that women don't care or won't spend money on an arousal product because they don't talk about sex with men. We could discuss that, according to research, sex takes a different order on women's priority lists. We could deliver a litany of straightforward, scientific, clinical facts and figures, all of which are true. But we knew from experience that those conversations would suck all the air out of the room and leave us with a cadre of more educated, but yawning, venture capitalists.

Sometimes, we actually felt like screaming at the top of our lungs, a la Cuba Gooding, Jr. as Rod Tidwell in *Jerry McGuire*, "Show me the money!"

Alternatively, we could refuse to take a time-out and seize control of the game by controlling the conversation.

Our $100 bill was a way to cut to the chase, shout "No time-outs," and roll—at top speed, with our eyes still on the ball—right past the "My wife has never brought this up" objection, or fly past sideways glances expressing investors' personal discomfort, right into creating the conversation that would elicit funds and drive our business growth. We always got around to presenting the evidence, to the numbers, to the size of the market. We just got there in our own time, in our own voices, and finally, in a manner of our own choosing.

Besides; time-outs can really, really mess up your rhythm.

...No Substitutions

So, how does *Rollerball* apply to entrepreneurship and specifically, my experiences as a person in the business of female sexual health? My dad would say, "Once you're in the game, you're in it to win it. You have to be 100 percent in it, you have to play hard, and even more importantly, you have to play fair. You have to go to work every day, work as hard and as smart as you can until you can't work anymore—and then get up the next day and do the same thing."

Case in point: The way ad approval worked seemed somewhat antiquated: Each television channel, whether or not it is owned by a major conglomerate, has its own Standards and Practices department, which must sign off on ads, and which places additional requirements and restrictions on them. For nine months in 2009, we banged our heads against Standards and Practices at nearly every outlet we tried to advertise with and met with only the most limited success. Most of the answers we got were resounding "Nos."

ABC, NBC, CBS—"No." WebMD—"No." Facebook—"Yes," for three short weeks, and then "No" (more on that later). TMZ (in my own personal estimation, the lowest form of TV life)—"No." ESPN, TNT, and all of their properties, said "No" at the beginning. The placements we *were* offered were inevitably during graveyard hours— overnights, in the wee hours of the morning. A few people may have been watching at that hour, but very few members of the target audience we had carefully defined and were trying to reach were.

And the few media channels we had been offered access to were not sufficient. They were not going to work for our business—in a new category, from a new company, starting a new conversation.

We knew we needed media—somehow. While public relations (or just PR, in the lingo of the business) is an amazing way to grow a company, you can't always predict that you will get coverage when, where, and how you need it. To have some control over our growth destiny, we needed to craft a message to achieve respectable growth in a reasonable period to make sure the company would be successful and deliver results to our investors. And we weren't about to accept any substitutions.

So, what did we do when 100-plus media outlets wouldn't take our advertising money for a female-oriented sexual health product even as they aired Cialis, Levitra, and Viagra ads by the truckload? It struck us that the fact that we couldn't buy media had to be, in fact, a story. If the Standards and Practices departments weren't going to let us *buy* media, we were going to *earn it* with public relations. So, we set out to find a PR firm that could work with us to turn initial media rejection into a story.

We wanted a partner that could get people to say the word "vagina" on television—not to make anybody uncomfortable, but to start a real conversation. This didn't happen overnight. It took us a year to find the right partner who thought that not being able to buy advertising was in fact, a story (shout-out here to the amazing Diane Terman, of Diane Terman Public Relations, who became that amazing partner).

Don't get mad, get even: *that was a story.* And it was a story that was tailor-made to appeal to precisely some of the same major media outlets that wouldn't take our ads. Their news and entertainment divisions were completely independent of their advertising divisions, after all.

In September 2010, the *New York Times* ran a story about the difficulty we had encountered with ad placement.[7] The very next morning, Zestra was discussed on *The View* and *Good Morning America* (thank you, Whoopi). The following week, Mary and I were interviewed on *Nightline,* which made me feel as if my life had come full circle. Ted Koppel, the legendary newsman and initial anchor for *Nightline,* had given the commencement speech at my Duke graduation, and I had been talking about it, quoting it, and writing about that speech for (gulp) thirty years.[8]

---

[7] Ellin, Abby. "For Female-Aphrodisiac Makers, Effort at Parity." *The New York Times.* September 13, 2010. http://www.nytimes.com/2010/09/14/business/media/14adco.html.

[8] Scherl, Rachel Braun. "Words to Live By, Graduates!" The Huffington Post. May 20, 2013. Accessed November 03, 2017. https://www.huffingtonpost.com/rachel-braun-scherl/words-to-live-by-graduates_b_3299145.html.

Eventually, based on the momentum of the story, we earned our way onto other outlets: every major newspaper in the country, every leading site, and major news stations. We were off to the races.

A funny aside: When the *San Francisco Chronicle* ran the story about our challenges with the media, it included the fact that WebMD had also ultimately refused to run the product's ads. We received a cease-and-desist letter from WebMD, which left us momentarily dumbstruck. But we politely—*very* politely—replied, "If you have information that suggests you did accept our ad, we would be delighted to retract our statement." Suffice it to say, we never heard back.

In the process of doing interviews and media to get the story out there, a realization slowly dawned on me; I loved this part of the job—creating the conversation, facing the challenges head-on. Not only that—I had passion about the subject. I was on fire about the ridiculous hypocrisy with which we, as a society and an economy, treat women's sexual health versus men's sexual health. Here was a subject that caused most people to trip over their tongues, and I was absolutely exhilarated when I talked about it. No euphemisms, no beating around the bush (so to speak), no infantilization of female sexuality for me; we were talking about grown women, and I was going to use my grown-up words to talk about their problems and their solutions. Someone had to stand up and say that the language of erectile dysfunction—"bigger, longer, stronger"—did not apply to women without adaptation or variation.

Also, not insignificantly, removing the shroud of mystery from sexuality and body parts doesn't *only* benefit women. In an era when we are finally beginning to address the epidemic of sexual assault, a body of research has concluded that when people know the proper names of reproductive body parts and understand what their bodies can do, this increases the chances that children, men, and women will report sexual violence and abuse. Being able to say, "He put his penis in my vagina" is especially important for children because it clarifies communication and also makes it clear that such incidents are not something to hide, according to Dr. Bob Sege, director of the division of family and child advocacy at Boston Medical Center.[9]

I was stumbling into my life's calling (because clearly the Olympic gymnastics career was not happening), one media story at a time.

The Women's Sexual Health and Wellness Industry Is Growing

It may come as a surprise (or not), but as recently as 1998, the state of Alabama was busy writing a new law against the sale of sex toys. Meanwhile, Texas's longstanding ban on such sales wasn't overturned as an unconstitutional intrusion on personal freedoms until 2008, which was the same year I coincidentally joined in this crusade myself. By 2016, with gradual but growing acceptance and public discussion of these products in shows like *Sex in the City* and narratives like *Fifty Shades of Grey,* the size of the pleasure product industry had reached $15 billion globally, with hundreds of manufacturers offering thousands of SKUs ranging from the most ancient designs to the most modern, high-end, technologically advanced devices.[10]

And that's just for starters.

There are global Vagipreneurs using technology, distribution, creativity, educational tools, and social transformation models to improve women's lives. From curing incontinence to providing

---

[9] Flam, Lisa. "Just Say 'vagina': Using Correct Body Part Names Empowers Kids, Experts Say." TODAY.com. April 23, 2013. https://www.today.com/parents/just-say-vagina-using-correct-body-part-names-empowers-kids-6C9551650.

[10] Burns, Janet. "How The 'Niche' Sex Toy Market Grew into An Unstoppable $15B Industry." *Forbes.* August 12, 2016. https://www.forbes.com/sites/janetwburns/2016/07/15/adult-expo-founders-talk-15b-sex-toy-industry-after-20-years-in-the-fray/#26fccd4e5bb9.

affordable alternatives to disposable tampons and pads, to teaching women how to achieve orgasm, remarkable things are happening out there right now, every day—economically empowering, environmentally trailblazing, taboo-demolishing things.

The space is continually defining and redefining itself. As of January 2017, CB Insights broke down the world of notable global feminine technology (or "Femtech") startups into an easy-to-digest chart. Clearly, given the pace of the change, this map changes quickly, as companies merge, fold, and are acquired. For this book, I interviewed several of the founders of companies included on the CB Insights map and beyond it.[11]

[11] The Femtech Market Map: 45+ Startups Focused On Women's Healthcare & Sexual Wellness." *CB Insights Research*. August 01, 2017. https://www.cbinsights.com/research/femtech-market-map/.

I've asked them to share their experiences, triumphs, frustrations, motivations, lessons, hopes, fears, joys, moments of levity, philosophies, and more. As trailblazers in the multi-billion-dollar global women's sexual health marketplace, these thought and market leaders are breaking down barriers with all the tools available to Vagipreneurs: unmet needs, awareness of those needs, fearlessness, honesty, humor, matter-of-factness, total conviction, and refusal to back down. Combined with the lessons I have learned and am still learning from these amazing trailblazers, I hope this book serves as both an inspiration and an early roadmap for others looking to take the plunge. This kind of societal transformation will and does take a village—and, most importantly, does not happen overnight.

So, get ready to get into the game. And remember the rules when things get serious: No time-outs. No substitutions. The Vagipreneurs profiled here certainly don't take any.

SECTION 2

The Female Sexual Satisfaction Marketplace Is on the Edge of Exploding

uilding any business is a challenge; building one that requires using words like "vagina," "breasts," "clitoris," "labia," "menstruation," or "female orgasm" generally means all of the old rules and bets are off. The story of trying to buy advertising for Zestra is a tiny microcosm of the systemic, society-wide resistance to launching such businesses.

Those barriers, along with fundraising obstacles and many others experienced by the entrepreneurs I interviewed (even problems finding qualified labor willing to work in the field of women's sexual and reproductive health), exist for many businesses in different forms. The fact remains that there are dozens, if not hundreds, of start-ups in the women's health and wellness space emerging in response to unmet needs and global demand. Because, let's face it; women have bodies, and bodies have needs. Where there's a need, there's a market. When there is a better solution, people look for it. And while these fierce start-up founders continue to make progress, many of the same barriers Mary and I faced still remain.

"It's a *niche* market," the objectors may say. How is 50 percent of the population a niche? I think what they really mean is that this stuff scares them. Women constitute nearly half of the global population (48.7 percent globally, 50.4 percent in the United States). This is a simple, undeniable, market-making fact. Let's face it; women (and their broad, varied, and complex health needs) aren't going anywhere.

The longer I live and work in this space, the more I am fascinated by it. For more than a year, I have invested hours, days, weeks (cumulatively, perhaps even months), interviewing dozens of innovative business leaders, creative thinkers, health care providers, and scientists. As I embarked on this project, I reached out to dozens of business founders and owners—a project I still continue to this day. I spoke with entrepreneurs I have had the pleasure of working with or meeting and others known to me only by the impact they have had. More still were recommended by the people who make up this unique community. I was pleasantly surprised; 95 percent of the people I reached out to responded and agreed to be interviewed.

I started with the premise that no one (or at least very few people) wake up and say, "I want to talk about vaginas for a living. I want to be in the business of female sexual health. *I want to be a Vagipreneur.*" That may be because while some of these businesses, by their very nature, generally begin the same way other start-ups do (as cold, hard, dollars-and-cents endeavors with a business plan and a solid, conventional, realistic marketing plan), others are born out of a need to find solutions to personal health problems.

Regardless of their origins, most Vagipreneurial businesses seem very quickly to become passion projects—sometimes prompting the entrepreneur to become positively evangelical or even missionary in style (no pun intended, honestly). That is not just because many founders are solving personal problems. And it is not just because many of the founders are women who are often characterized as being "emotional" (which is a dirty word in business). The reason is simply because to do anything well, and certainly to do anything that is *challenging* well, you need passion, persistence, and perseverance when people are continually trying to knock you off balance, off your feet, and out of the ring—over and over and over again. (As I write, I have visions of Sylvester Stallone as Rocky Balboa screaming in the final minutes of *Rocky*, "Cut me, Mick," so that he can see well enough to get back into the ring with Apollo Creed. *Rocky* is another entrepreneurial success story, by the way—an Oscar-winning film written by a then-unknown thirty-year-old actor who created his own opportunity when he wasn't finding or landing the kinds of roles he wanted to play.)

Succeeding in the crazy, upside-down Vagipreneurial space doesn't necessarily require *different* skill sets, dedication, or drive than it takes to succeed in any other start-up. But often, it *does* require *extraordinary amounts* of those resources. Most entrepreneurs I know wake up each morning filled with hope and drive that today is the day their vision will explode, that others will see and grasp what they are building. Each is conscious of limited resources—money, time, energy. Each has the ability to work long, hard days with very little recognition or signs of progress. Of course, at points in the process, and regardless of the ultimate success of the company, many face the tough but realistic awareness that despite all of their time, effort, and money, their companies might not have the ultimate success or impact they hope. Or that their efforts may *never* lead to a huge payday or ringing the opening bell on the New York Stock Exchange one day.

Most new businesses end up requiring more time and cash than their founders initially thought they might need to succeed, but in Vagipreneurial businesses, timelines tend to be even more elongated. And with a couple of notable exceptions (such as the sale of Sprout Pharmaceuticals and its flagship product, Addyi—a feminine libido-enhancing pharmaceutical drug—to Valeant, for one—and that is a whole different story), the headline-making exits for Vagipreneurs have been very few and far between.

But today and every day, Vagipreneurs are out there making noise, and the crescendo is getting louder and louder.

So what have I learned as I spoke to these business leaders? What have their experiences, combined with my own, imparted for those who are thinking about striking out in the entrepreneurial space?

Many members of this new generation of entrepreneurs experience the same frustrations, barriers, and late-night worries that my partner and I did during our fundraising meetings. Different standards are applied when products and services are sold to women to be used on body parts that are normally hidden by bras and underwear. That's an undeniable fact. But there is so much to be learned from these pioneers.

- **There are many paths to success**, and with products and services that are centered on women's sexual health and wellness, the path may be over, under, or around the most direct route to the goal. You don't have to *like* these extra barriers and double-standards, but to succeed, you'll have to acknowledge them and find ways to circumvent them—and be prepared ahead of time for the extra distance that may be added to your trip.

- **Never, ever, *ever* take "No" for an answer.** You may hear "No" a dozen times. You may hear it a hundred. But somewhere out there is your "Yes," and if you stop before you get there, somebody else will hear it—not you. Many of the Vagipreneurs interviewed in the coming chapters describe doors slamming (both literally and proverbially) in their faces—until they finally met the right funder/partner/savior who "got it," who took a chance on them and their businesses.

- **It's not only OK to ask for help from people who have fought the same battles—it's a best practice.** You can preserve sanity, time, and precious resources if you can turn to others in your industry as a business brain trust, or if you can find leaders in other industries who faced years of pushback before they made progress against older, prevailing ways of doing things against strong headwinds.

- **Somebody has to be first to market.** *It may as well be you.* Somebody has to break through the front lines of inertia, inaction, and insufficiency. Today, in an increasingly paperless world, we can hardly imagine what life was like without computers and smart devices, before they existed. Today, you could probably convince some people to give up one of their lungs before they'd hand over their smartphone even for a few days. I don't think Mrs. Lieb, my eighth-grade typing teacher, could ever have imagined a world in which we didn't have to use filmy white correction tape and backspaces to eliminate mistakes. Do you have any recollection of life before your cell phone, when you could only be reached at your desk or at home, or when you sometimes got a busy signal if the person you wanted to call was already using the landline? Can you remember exactly when you first saw something labeled "gluten-free" on a grocery store shelf? A few years ago, nobody thought driverless vehicles would amount to much, and now we're talking about *when*, not *if,* they will arrive on our nation's highways carrying freight and passengers.

- **Never, ever lose your sense of humor or sense of perspective.** I often think of several famous lines from one of my all-time favorite movies, *Airplane*. As events start to go terribly wrong and it appears a plane crash is imminent, the chief air traffic controller, masterfully played by Lloyd Bridges, says, "Looks like I picked the wrong week to stop smoking." And he lights up. At the next crisis point, he says, "Looks like

I picked the wrong week to stop drinking." Commence the pour. Finally, "Looks like I picked the wrong week to stop sniffing glue." Many were the days when that sentiment described how I felt during my own journey, and tapping into humor kept me from becoming totally discouraged.

- **Make sure you have a thick (massively thick) skin and effective coping mechanisms.** If you choose to go into a Vagipreneurial endeavor, you will, with terrifying certainty and predictable regularity, hear offensive comments. You will hear inappropriate observations. You will hear disparaging and discouraging feedback. You will find yourself in meetings that only the Harvey Weinsteins of the world would feel comfortable in. You might find yourself on the receiving end of demeaning, sometimes even insulting remarks about you, your product, and the future prospects for your business. You may even be attacked by online trolls for your appearance (stay tuned). When that happens (and it will happen), you will need to dig deep and *find your own coping mechanism*. I always choose humor—anything that makes me laugh out loud, hard, and puts me at risk for a little accident (more on incontinence later). Some people enjoy humorous books, comics, and essays; others may have favorite go-to, laugh-out-loud, standup comedians they can turn to in times of stress; yet others may be able to rely on a solid lineup of bookmarked websites or a streaming queue full of reliable programs. For me, when I'm experiencing a momentary aggravation that I know I can't respond to in kind, I think of my favorite funny scenes and quotes from classic slapstick movies (*Wedding Crashers, The Hangover, Animal House,* whatever). It does help, in my case, that I literally can laugh at the same scenes endlessly. Regardless of your own coping strategy, you must have one—to get through the journey in one piece, to keep you grounded and to keep you smiling through the pain and pleasures of forging a new path through this unexplored forest of opportunities.

Meet the Vagipreneurs

As I interviewed the Vagipreneurs profiled throughout this book, I used a singular questionnaire to structure the discussions. The interviews led off with the catalyzing moment when these business leaders found their idea, stumbled into this passion, and each interview eventually ended with French television personality Bernard Pivot's famous ten-question script, generally more familiar to Americans as James Lipton's closing queries to every guest on *Inside the Actors Studio.*[12]

I structured the interviews this way because I wanted to maintain a similar overall shape to each discussion while I gained insights on both the personal and the professional perspectives of the individual Vagipreneur. I did not merely want them to tell a business story— of sales, supply chains, fundraising—but to delve more deeply into how all of these elements made their journeys fully human. I wanted to know their personal stories, their histories, their motivations. I wanted to learn about what had set them on their paths, the potential roadblocks they had encountered, the detours they had taken, and their workarounds, as well as their inspiration, motivation, and glimpses of the successes, setbacks, and failures they had experienced along the way.

---

[12] Lipton, James. *Inside the Actors Studio*, Bravo, 1994.

And because it's only fair, before I share my interview subjects' answers to Pivot's ten questions in the rest of the book, here are my own.

THE QUESTIONS

Rachel Braun Scherl, Vagipreneur, Author, Marketing Strategist and Business Builder, Speaker

- **What is your favorite word?**
  Yes.

- **What is your least favorite word?**
  Loser.

- **What turns you on creatively, spiritually, or emotionally?**
  Being with family and friends and laughing until I can't breathe.

- **What turns you off creatively, spiritually, or emotionally?**
  Hypocrisy, violence, lack of compassion, and unwillingness to take responsibility for your actions.

- **What sound or noise do you love?**
  Laughter.

- **What sound or noise do you hate?**
  Chalk on a blackboard or a car honking, unless I am the one honking.

- **What is your favorite curse word?**
  Fuck (kids, I know I told you not to sound crass, but sometimes you just have to use it).

- **What profession other than your own would you like to attempt?**
  Talk show host.

- **What profession would you not like to do?**
  Garbage collector. I have a serious germ problem.

- **If Heaven exists, what would you like to hear God say when you arrive at the Pearly Gates?**
  Congratulations, you were picked first for the coed softball team!

CHAPTER 3

Technology: Delivering Women's Sexual Health and Wellness through Technical Solutions

Tech: It's not just for millennials. And sex tech is definitely not just for millennials.

When I talk about technological solutions for women's sexual and reproductive health and wellness, I'm using the word "technology" in both specific and broad ways. I am not only talking about devices, microchips, apps, or the internet of things; I am also talking specifically about novel devices, new formulations, and new combinations of existing ingredients put together in different ways.

It's the idea and the goal that drives these solutions. Did the Vagipreneur get into business to solve women's unique problems through novel, more advanced, easier-to-use, automated, or more reliable methods? Does the product deliver results through highly engineered solutions that are created, tested, validated, certified, calibrated, or verified through rigorous scientific or medical processes?

There's not much in the modern, developed world that hasn't been lured into the world of tech, and it's happened so rapidly, we've almost forgotten that only ten years ago, we didn't carry the entire world's accumulated knowledge with us in our pockets or pocketbooks. (By the way, does anybody actually say "pocketbook" when they mean "purse" or "bag" anymore, like our grandmothers did? Or did *Sex in the City* exterminate that word from the common vocabulary? And speaking of the word "purse," if you didn't already know it's a euphemism for "vagina" that dates back to 1538, you can tick *learn something new today* off your to-do list. There are a lot of those euphemisms—some quaint, some amusing, some not so amusing.)

Let's meet our first Vagipreneur.

✳ LISA LEVIN: Former Marketing Director, Veru Health Care

"The most inspiring moment for me was going to the international AIDS convention. The female condom is not just female-oriented. This is human-oriented."

It takes a lot of *chutzpah* to walk away from a giant, global conglomerate and into a women-focused business selling a product very few people know about, especially when it's more expensive than the long-established male-oriented version. But if anybody can help to increase the adoption and use rates of the female condom worldwide, it's people like Lisa Levin, who are fiercely unafraid to step up and evangelize for its place in women's sexual health when men don't—or won't—exercise their own option.

Lisa is the former director of marketing for The Female Health Company (now known as Veru, a new entity born in 2017 when the company acquired Aspen Park Pharmaceuticals). Veru, like The Female Health Company before it, manufactures a female condom called FC2.

Lisa comes from a family that's no stranger to the world of business. While she always wanted to be involved in doing good and helping people, it simply never occurred to her to become a nurse or a social worker. She instead looked at her dad, in his role as a chief financial officer (CFO), and realized very early that she had the same mind for business.

She joined the world of Vagipreneurship after a long and successful career at Kraft Foods and their agencies. "Honestly, I was burned out on the consumer space and salad dressing and snacks and the corporate environment," Levin says. "I had worked in that world for twenty years, ever since I had graduated from school. I'd made a pretty big name for myself. But it wasn't enough." So she took some time off, donating her time at a brand new café started by a friend in her hometown of Evanston, IL, which also employed and trained at-risk youth who had come out of the criminal justice system and needed to develop marketable job skills. That experience was the catalyst she needed: her next paid position, she decided, would be one that empowered people.

A temporary agency put her in touch with The Female Health Company before it was known as Veru, and the rest, as they say, is history. Bringing FC2 to life was a hard-fought effort, requiring six years and $12 million to develop the product and many fits and starts to navigate the regulatory process.

Part of the challenge was that, while the male condom is considered a Class II medical device, the female condom, because it is inserted into the woman's body, had to go through the more arduous Class III medical device approval process, which required studies that had not been anticipated. Interestingly, the initial mission envisioned for the female condom was not as a commercial enterprise, but more as a much-needed choice for women in developing countries—both for pregnancy protection and disease prevention.

While at least six different female condom manufacturers and form factors now exist, (including at least one that's contained within an entire pair of underwear—*sexy*), Veru has been around for the longest. Its polyurethane FC1 launched in 1992 in the United

Kingdom and 1993 in the United States after the device secured initial Food and Drug Administration (FDA) approval.

But there were issues with the product's design. Early users of the first-generation female condom (which is essentially a looser-fitting version of a condom designed to line the vagina, held in place by an outer ring that sits outside the vagina and an inner ring that is inserted over the cervix) couldn't help but notice it made rustling, squeaky noises during sexual intercourse. That's the nature of polyurethane. And as most women know, distractions during sex are the last thing many of them need during the journey to orgasm (if in fact they are not part of the one-third of women who never experience them).

In 2006, the new and improved FC2 was introduced, using medical-grade nitrile instead of polyurethane—the same material physicians' exam gloves are made of, and it significantly improved sensation with the FC2 as well as eliminating those rustling sounds.

When Levin joined the company in 2015, she says, everybody at the company had expertise in sales and pharmaceuticals, but there was no in-house expertise in marketing. She entered the organization with fresh eyes and a new approach. "Some people were asking, 'Should we offer a version of the product that's studded, like male condoms?' But we knew that wasn't where we wanted or needed to go with this product. The female condom exists because it can make a very real difference in the world; male condoms serve one purpose, and female condoms exist for women's needs. It exists because a lot of men don't want to use condoms, for whatever the reasons. We know condoms save lives. The female condom is empowerment. It's freedom. It not only prevents pregnancy in a way that's hormone-free and good for your body, but it also prevents the transmission of sexually transmitted diseases like AIDS and Zika virus, which can cause catastrophic harm to children in utero." And as STIs increase in the older population, the female condom is finding another important audience.

Levin's role and passion might have caused others to blush, but not her. "Almost everybody I've ever talked to about what I was doing was quite frankly blown away. They were fascinated. 'A condom for vaginas? That is so cool.' It makes for very interesting dinner table conversation. On the other hand, during market research, one of the most interesting moments for me was during a focus group we did with a book group consisting of twenty best friends. They were initially quite shy and didn't want to talk about the device. But once they loosened up and started chatting, one of them asked, 'Can you throw it up out of your mouth?' That made me realize a lot of women *really* don't understand how our bodies work. We have a long way to go, still."

Boy, do we ever. On December 1, 2017, the United States FDA *finally* announced proposed changes that would reclassify single-use female condoms on par with male condoms, from Class III to Class II devices, removing the high barrier to market entry for development and sale of new such devices. It's a move that has been more than twenty-five years in the making. And the new changes are still in the proposal stage—in today's uncertain healthcare environment, still far from a slam-dunk.[13]

---

[13] "Obstetrical and Gynecological Devices; Reclassification of Single-Use Female Condom, To Be Renamed Single-Use Internal Condom." *Federal Register.* December 04, 2017. https://www.federalregister.gov/documents/2017/12/04/2017-26011/obstetrical-and-gynecological-devices-reclassification-of-single-use-female-condom-to-be-renamed.

Lisa says her proudest moment in the work was being able to say that 450,000 female condoms were distributed in the 2016 Olympic Village in Rio, and 100,000 were FC2s.

THE QUESTIONS

Lisa Levin, Former Marketing Director, The Female Health Company

- **What is your favorite word?**
  Chameleon.

- **What is your least favorite word?**
  Retard.

- **What turns you on creatively, spiritually, or emotionally?**
  Music. It's very spiritual to me and for me. Synagogue and services are empty without music, for example. Actively creating music also expands my creative perspective— working in a group, teamwork, brainstorming, working in a collaborative environment.

- **What turns you off creatively, spiritually, or emotionally?**
  Working in a silo and mean people.

- **What sound or noise do you love?**
  The rain on a rooftop.

- **What sound or noise do you hate?**
  A fork on teeth.

- **What is your favorite curse word?**
  Asshat.

- **What profession other than your own would you like to attempt?**
  Social worker.

- **What profession would you not like to do?**
  Accountant.

- **If Heaven exists, what would you like to hear God say when you arrive at the Pearly Gates?**
  "You did good. Do good."

✳ KAREN LONG: Cofounder, Nuelle, Inc.

"The stories of sadness, loss, and despair over not having the physical or emotional feelings of desire they wished they had, were profound. I knew I wanted to help. Our early clinical work showed what a difference in relationships, self-esteem, and women's well-being the product could make, so I gladly joined the team and the mission."

On the opposite end of the spectrum of the avoidance or protective sex like the female condom are technological solutions for women who aren't currently having as much sex or enjoying it as they once did, or would like to potentially have more and enjoy it more.

There are gaps between the genders when it comes to sexual enjoyment and fulfillment. One is the orgasm gap; men do actually have more orgasms than women, empirically speaking, and it isn't even a photo finish. According to the National Survey of Sexual Health and Behavior, a comprehensive study, 91 percent of males report they made it across the line in their last sexual encounter, compared to 64 percent of women.[14] But another problematic breach

---

[14] Chalabi, Mona. "The Gender Orgasm Gap." *FiveThirtyEight*, 12 Apr. 2016, fivethirtyeight.com/features/the-gender-orgasm-gap/.

between the genders is the *perception gap*; men think their partners have more orgasms than they actually do. And this gap is *also* wide. In the same survey, 85 percent of men reported their previous sexual partner had experienced orgasm. Since we know only 64 percent of women affirmatively stated, "yes, I did," to the same researchers, that's quite a mismatch. (To be fair, a great deal of this gap is caused by differences in physiology. Men's sexual response and orgasm is a much simpler endeavor than women's, as we've discussed.)

Enter Nuelle, a women's health and wellness company that was founded to design scientifically sound solutions for women who struggle with arousal and desire for sexual intimacy. "The concept that these problems are rarely discussed, and are real and profound, was brought to our attention by a male urologist," Nuelle cofounder Karen Long explains. "At a urology medical meeting, a specialist was talking to one of our founders, Dr. Josh Makower, and another colleague about male sexual health and BPH (benign prostatic hyperplasia) solutions and he asked, 'Have you ever thought about researching and creating solutions for female sexual concerns, such as changes in arousal and desire with aging?' As a urologist, I am fixing up all these men later in life, but there is a partner on the other side who is none too pleased. We have men ready to go to the dance and they have no dance partner. In other words, no one is looking at the fact that once a male's issues were 'fixed,' there was a female partner who had her own concerns and no ready solutions."

That was the spark for the research and then the development of Nuelle's flagship product, Fiera, which is a compact, elegant device that was designed to be used by women *before* sex to increase both arousal and interest. It creates physical arousal through vibration and gentle suction, thereby creating blood flow, and its ability to do so has been consistently and repeatedly scientifically validated.

Long says two things helped her make the decision as she was considering whether to go into the women's sexual wellness space. The first was that, in an era when four-hour erections are casually mentioned in those aforementioned side-by-side bathtub ads during football games, "we still do not talk about women's needs without shame or guilt or that familiar, uncomfortable giggle. But these needs or concerns are affecting quality-of-life. I felt almost an obligation each time I saw the commercials to take a stand and provide a voice and the best possible product we could to make a difference. The second was our early work with women. The stories of sadness, loss, and despair over not having the physical or emotional feelings of desire they wished they had were profound. I knew I wanted to help. Our early clinical work showed what a difference in relationships, self-esteem, and women's well-being the product could make, so I gladly joined the team and the mission."

Long is a crusader when it comes to removing the tenacious veil of shame from women's sexual health. To combat the messages many women hear growing up about not only sex but their bodies, Long and Nuelle crafted a humorous viral social campaign called "Legalize V," encouraging women to throw away the "polite" but stigma-reinforcing words women are taught to substitute for "vagina," like "hoo-ha," "vajayjay," "poonani," and so on.[15] (Because Vagipreneurial royalty is tightly interconnected, many of the women who participated in the video for the Legalize V campaign are included in this book: Alexandra Fine, Jordana Kier, Colette Courtion, and Wendy Strgar all lent their enthusiastic support to the cause.)

---

[15] Legalize V. "Legalize V". Filmed [October 2016]. YouTube video, 1:32. Posted [October 2016]. https://www.youtube.com/watch?v=juFirUtedE4.

Long says that even though her "tribe" is people in health care, the most challenging aspect of developing Fiera was getting beyond the embarrassment factor in both men and women: she includes herself among them. "Initially, yes, I did have to get over my discomfort discussing these issues when talking about Nuelle, and what I discovered was that the clearer and more direct I was, the better and more constructive my conversations became. I found if I approached the topic as an educator, I became a lot more fearless. Some women are naturally brave, and others are more naturally inhibited by the culture around us. When you speak as an educator and an advocate, it's very difficult to be afraid. And that created a snowball effect; the more I spoke about these issues, which are very real problems for women who are going through menopause or who have lost desire because of treatment for breast cancer, the more I realized this problem affects people I know. Friends and family, underdogs who weren't being listened to. That made me want to do even more and make a difference for women who don't have a voice, because I had a voice and I could speak for them."

Long's advice for others who are considering Vagipreneurship is that it becomes a mission, and you absolutely have to believe in what you're doing right down to the core of your being. "It's not for the faint of heart, leading and starting companies in this space, in the face of all the societal stigmas," Long says, "but I am happy to report that many young women today are taking the challenge head on."

In 2017, Nuelle's leaders realized they would need a larger coalition to spearhead the challenge of getting the message out to women. Through market research, they also learned that these conversations are still quite private and taking place in a woman's doctor's office, if they are happening anywhere. So Nuelle decided it would enlist the health care community to help spread the word about Fiera.

Nuelle was sold in mid-2017 to a pharmaceutical company that has made male and female sexual health its core focus. Starting in 2018, the Fiera product has a dedicated sales force talking about the benefits of sexual health. Long is happy the conversation is being had, even if, for now, it is only in the doctor's office. It's a great start.

THE QUESTIONS

Karen Long, Cofounder, Nuelle

- **What is your favorite word?**
  Persistence.

- **What is your least favorite word?**
  No.

- **What turns you on creatively, spiritually, or emotionally?**
  Open dialogue and trust.

- **What turns you off creatively, spiritually, or emotionally?**
  Dishonesty.

- **What sound or noise do you love?**
  Children's laughter.

- **What sound or noise do you hate?**
  Snoring.

- **What is your favorite curse word?**
  Fuck (especially when I hear, "No").

- **What profession other than your own would you like to attempt?**
  Professional chef or home designer; something really creative.

- **What profession would you not like to do?**
  Professional politician.

- **If heaven exists, what would you like to hear God say when you arrive at the Pearly Gates?**
  "The work you did; it made a difference."

✳ HOLLY ROCKWEILER: Cofounder and CEO, Madorra

"What are all of the things estrogen does in the body, and specifically within the vagina? Eventually, we zeroed in on blood flow. So, what were other ways we could induce vaginal blood flow without hormones?"

In April 2017, seventy-four of Portland's most ambitious startups gathered for TechfestNW, a competitive pitch-fest in which emerging businesses in a wild array of categories, from baby food to electronic payment systems, duked it out for both bragging rights and a not-insignificant chunk of funding.[16] At the end of the day (literally—it was a one-day event), the winner was Madorra, a company developing a handheld ultrasound device to treat post-menopausal vaginal dryness without hormones.

Beating out businesses in virtual reality and bot-coding was not

---

[16] Schmid, Thacher. "The Best Startup Pitch in Town? A Portland-Based Company That Soothes the Symptoms of Menopause." *Willamette Week*. March 24, 2017. http://www.wweek.com/technology/2017/03/24/the-best-startup-pitch-in-town-a-portland-based-company-that-soothes-the-symptoms-of-menopause/.

just professionally rewarding for Holly Rockweiler, the company's cofounder and CEO, but also personally satisfying. "I am a biomedical engineer by training, and originally I worked in the cardiac space, but I didn't love the big company experience," Holly explains. "I've always had this philosophy that if you don't like what you're doing, you should try doing the exact opposite. So, I went into the Stanford Biodesign Fellowship program, a one-year intensive curriculum in medical device innovation. Many people who go through that program do start companies afterward, but that wasn't my original goal. The program begins by teaching you to look for unmet needs in specific clinical areas. And when my team and I started looking at unmet needs, I realized women's health was high on the list.

"There were a lot of reasons that made nonhormonal treatment of vaginal dryness an attractive project. For one, it's an incredibly common theme for women. It's a huge, untapped potential market. When we dug in and started doing background research, we realized there was very little recent literature on the topic. Once the need was identified, there's been a groundswell of support for it—anybody I've talked to within the women's health community has been enthusiastic and incredibly encouraging, which has been critical during the company's start-up period."

Holly began laying the foundation for the company and the product with her small Stanford biodesign team; three engineers and one physician. They were focused like lasers on meeting the physical needs of women whose own bodies have stopped producing the hormones necessary for adequate vaginal lubrication. "One of our initial catalysts for developing a nonhormonal product was women who have survived breast cancer," Holly says. "Many are younger women, going through rapidly induced chemical menopause, long before their friends. They may not know where to turn for advice or help. They cannot use existing, hormonal solutions for vaginal dryness. Those solutions are contraindicated because hormones, in many cases, could cause a recurrence of cancer. And younger women often aren't comfortable with over-the-counter products, not only because they contain unpronounceable chemicals, but also because they aren't effective enough to relieve symptoms. There were, we found, a lot of layers of this onion. Developing our device required understanding the problem thoroughly before diving headlong into developing the solution."

Holly and her partners also knew there is a rising demographic tide of women who are looking for relief from the vaginal symptoms of natural menopause; estrogen declines as women age and the team did a great deal of research on both the causes and symptoms of vaginal dryness in menopause. "What are all of the things estrogen does in the body, and specifically within the vagina? Eventually, we zeroed in on blood flow. So, we wondered, what were *other* ways we could induce vaginal blood flow *without* hormones?"

Holly gives full credit to her training at Stanford. The biodesign program taught her the number one rule of product design is, "Ask your user," and so the design team went out and did just that. They spoke with representatives from their target market, conducting one-on-one interviews, doing market surveys, and incorporating clinical research at appropriate junctures during product development. What were the must-haves? What were the nice-to-haves? Who is the woman who would be willing—even eager—to use an ultrasonic device at home to improve vaginal blood flow and treat vaginal dryness?

Throughout the process of bringing the company and the

device to life, Holly, like nearly every Vagipreneur I've spoken with, experienced awkward conversations that expose the need for more candid dialogue about unmet needs in women's health and where women-centered products can take center stage.

"There was an incredible moment when I was speaking with a young guy who works at a millennial venture capital firm. I was describing our device. He asked, 'Is it a lot like penis size?' I was speechless. Why would a woman's product be about a *penis*? Sometimes men define their self-worth around penis size; I get that. But do women define themselves around how wet they get? I'm not sure, but I don't think it was relevant to our conversation."

Six months after Madorra's big win at Portland's pitch-fest, the company is well positioned for more success. It had its third birthday in the summer of 2017, complete with cake and champagne. It has raised two rounds of funding, including grants from the National Science Foundation, and with those early funds, the device went through early clinical feasibility testing. At the moment, the next mountain to scale is FDA approval, for which the company is raising Series A funding. "This is the stuff that's one of our biggest headwinds," Holly says, "because there haven't been a lot of VC-level exits in women's health in the past few years. But so far so good. And it has been absolutely exhilarating to be around the table with people who understand the science, women's needs, and the FDA. As a first-time entrepreneur, it's been an eye-opening and thrilling process to be a part of."

As they say in the *Star Wars* universe, "May the Force be with her!"

THE QUESTIONS

Holly Rockweiler, Cofounder and CEO, Madorra

- **What is your favorite word?**
  Pamplemousse, *which is French for grapefruit.*

- **What is your least favorite word?**
  No.

- **What turns you on creatively, spiritually, or emotionally?**
  Creatively: A big piece of white paper and markers. Spiritually: Nature, hiking trails. Emotionally: Best friends and my husband.

- **What turns you off creatively, spiritually, or emotionally?**
  Stress makes it hard to do anything well. Then I get detail-oriented and don't see the big picture and don't reach out to friends when I need to.

- **What sound or noise do you love?**
  Peaceful quiet, which I experienced on vacation in Iceland; you can't hear anything but the waves rippling.

- **What sound or noise do you hate?**
  Yelling. My husband watches this show, Archer, but I can't handle it because people are constantly yelling at each other.

- **What is your favorite curse word?**
  Fuck.

- **What profession other than your own would you like to attempt?**
  In my next life, I want to be a cultural anthropologist— study organizational behavior, figure out why culture at

some companies is so good and in others so bad. Does it have to be bad if it is big?

- **What profession would you not like to do?**
  Food service.

- **If heaven exists, what would you like to hear God say when you arrive at the Pearly Gates?**
  "The party started."

CHAPTER 4

Distribution: Bringing More Products to More Women in More Places

I'm probably not telling you anything you don't know when I say that disruption in distribution models have quite possibly defined the opening years of the twenty-first century. Amazon got the ball rolling, first with books, but then with the vision: why not sell…well, everything? Online? And deliver it to consumers' homes? The rise of online shopping is still growing, and in 2016 Americans reached a new benchmark: According to an annual joint survey by analytics firm comScore and UPS, more people now purchase more things online (51 percent) than they do in stores (49 percent).[17] With a double-whammy of free returns at many online retailers and the ability to shop for the lowest possible price, there's less and less incentive to head out to the wilds, where other predators are stalking the same prey (and there's no parking, and the traffic, and let's face it, putting on a full face of makeup and a bra is something that just isn't worth the hassle some days).

Speaking of bras: Back in the 1970s, I was the kind of kid who read the newspaper cover-to-cover, including the classified ads, if you can believe that. And in the personal section, I was always intrigued by one ad that was tucked away there and didn't seem to fit. It was very brief, and it wasn't an ad for a Man Seeking Woman, a

---

[17] Farber, Madeline. "Consumers Are Now Doing Most of Their Shopping Online." *Fortune*, 8 June 2016, http://fortune.com/2016/06/08/online-shopping-increases/.

Woman Seeking Man, or any other permutation of Human Seeking Human. It was a couple of brief lines of text, and it advertised the availability of post-mastectomy bras at a local retailer. Now, as a child, I didn't know what a mastectomy was. But I knew what a bra was, I knew that the personal ads were a grown-up section of the newspaper, and I wasn't sure that I was supposed to be reading them. The ads were hidden most likely as a result of the enormous social stigma surrounding breast cancer at that time.

All of this is to say, novel approaches to distribution are changing the shopping experience—and it's more than time. Especially when it comes to women's bodies, the shopping experience hasn't always been a pleasant one. So anything that Vagipreneurs are doing in the space to improve how we can select, personalize, tailor, customize, and make the shopping and delivery of products we need for our health and comfort, the better.

The best businesses emerging in this space create experiences that are genuinely pleasant and personalized; at a minimum, they are streamlined, convenient, and maybe even enjoyable. You order, and you get exactly what you expected, with no problems and no glitches.

✳ JANET KRAUS: CEO and Cofounder, peach

> *"Objectification is one of the leading reasons why women are in positions of less power."*

Janet Kraus is no stranger to entrepreneurship. In fact, she's taught it. At *Harvard*. And she sits on three start-up boards.

So, it's probably no surprise that peach (the name of which is intentionally styled that way, with a lowercase *p*)—a women's clothing company she serves as CEO and cofounder—is on the leading edge right now. And although the business model is continually evolving, it all began with bras—literally the foundation of a woman's wardrobe. Originally founded with the idea of building a personalized, coordinated wardrobe that begins with a well fitting bra, peach began the sales cycle with an in-person or virtual meeting with a personal stylist (sales representative) who used a multiplicity of individual measurements to find exactly the right support to match a woman's size, shape, and lift/shaping needs.

It was a far cry from the headache-inducing experience of shopping at national chains that sell lacy, stringy, excessively padded, yet maddeningly unsupportive undergarments that seem designed to appeal more to men in bedrooms than to provide reliable, smooth, consistent support for women under their clothes in boardrooms. That's exactly the experience Janet had in mind when she founded peach.

And then there are the clothes—soft, relaxed, comfortable, many with the forgiving ease of elasticized waists, which customers love, but at the same time elegant and flowing, put together and presented on the company's website as seasonal "stories" or capsule wardrobes rather than "collections." Janet, as many others do, calls this category "athleisure," the kind of crossover wardrobe that can straddle work and play—and that is what peach creates and sells. "I'd say 25 percent of our clothing you can actually work out in, and the rest are thoroughly appropriate for a casual work environment. We take our inspiration from the runway, but all fifteen pieces from each season mix and match and create incredible possibilities."

In December 2016, with 500 active stylists in the field, Janet made the data-driven decision to focus on the products that were making the most revenue for stylists and the company. She was committed to creating economic opportunities for women above everything else, so she moved the emphasis of peach from time-consuming intimate fittings to the athleisure line; while bras are still available, they are no longer the first stop in peach's sales funnel.

"My Mom always said you have two ears and one mouth for a reason," she says, "and our stylists were telling us they needed the right size check in their pocket for the amount of time they were putting into their sales efforts. Also, you start a business with a hypothesis; it will be hard. After two years, though, the friction should be reduced. If somebody has been on the job two months and says she's still learning, that's expected. If she's been doing it two years and she still isn't over the learning curve? Something needs to change. So, we listened and we made adjustments. As an entrepreneur, change can happen *ridiculously fast*. Sometimes it needs to." She lost her mother in the summer of 2017, adding an extra layer of poignancy to those words to live by.

"Working with a peach stylist is designed from end-to-end to be confidence-building," says Janet. "You shop in your own home, in a supportive and caring environment in which you are totally comfortable. There are no harsh, strange, greenish fluorescent lights. There's no pressure to get in and get out of a dressing room, no oddly distorted 360-degree mirrors. Our stylists are supportive, caring, and passionate about creating a positive experience for women. Ultimately I want to do for women and their wardrobes what Uber and Lyft did for taxis; for decades, we rode around in the backs of these broken-down, bumpy, smelly, uncomfortable vehicles and we all thought that was just the way things were, and we overpaid for that 'privilege.' Then along came ridesharing services, and suddenly we realized getting from one place to the other could not only be more affordable—it could actually be fun and delightful!"[18]

The company's relaunch and change in product lineup also required a change in the product team, and Janet was able to attract talent from Under Armour's women's apparel line and Victoria's Secret Sport. The fabrics peach is working with now as they develop their seasonal capsule wardrobes are leading-edge, straight out of the performance world—tough yet lightweight, appropriate for gym, work, and play.

The distribution model that employs stylists also empowers the women peach employs as sales associates, and that is as important to Janet as tending to the hearts and physical needs of her end customers. "When she works with customers in their homes, our stylist has a life-changing experience. Eighteen percent of our customers say they've made friends through peach."

Janet says peach is her life's calling. "I could help ninety women at a time teaching entrepreneurship at Harvard, or I could impact thousands of women through this company. The mission is ultimately similar."

Like so many woman entrepreneurs, Janet found herself fundraising during the company's start-up phase pitching the idea of peach to men, and, like so many others, found herself being told, "This isn't a problem because…" (I told you to wait for it) "… women love to shop." *For lingerie.* "It was all I could do not to let my jaw physically drop," Janet says. "What arrogance. Who are you, gentlemen, to assert, with such absolute certainty—such astonishing and baseless self-assured arrogance—how women feel about

---

[18] Note: I interviewed Janet Kraus before news broke about Uber's treatment of female employees and subsequent shake-ups in the company's management as well as and board dismissals.

shopping for lingerie? Or that women 'love' Victoria's Secret? How could you *possibly know that*?"

But she is, above all, an exceedingly practical woman. "It's not helpful to your case, when you are raising money, to argue against yourself, and pointing fingers doesn't help," Janet says. "In fact, one of the acts I've found that can help women entrepreneurs is to reach out and find male mentors who have made money with venture capitalists. If you are out to build a game-changing company, you will need tens of millions of dollars in support to get there. You don't need access. You don't need somebody to simply open the door for you. You need advice, championship—advocacy."

For Janet, women's bodies and empowering them is not just a business mission; it's personal. She has twin 11-year-old daughters, and she wants them to grow up in a world in which they feel great about their bodies, no matter what. "There was a time in my own life," Janet admits, "when I was basically anorexic. I self-destructed for years and years. I don't know why we think being excessively thin is a good idea, but for a long time, it earned me praise, and that was terribly unhealthy. I want to actively work on creating a world in which *every* girl has a positive self-image, without body shame, no matter her size or shape. Objectification is one of the leading reasons why women are in positions of less power."

THE QUESTIONS

Janet Kraus, Cofounder, peach

- **What is your favorite word?**
  Love, followed closely by peach.

- **What is your least favorite word?**
  Hate.

- **What turns you on creatively, spiritually, or emotionally?**
  Nature and music (I'm a vocalist—a singer/songwriter).

- **What turns you off creatively, spiritually, or emotionally?**
  Rain.

- **What sound or noise do you love?**
  The ocean.

- **What sound or noise do you hate?**
  Traffic.

- **What is your favorite curse word?**
  Fuck.

- **What profession other than your own would you like to attempt?**
  Comedian.

- **What profession would you not like to do?**
  Optometrist.

- **If Heaven exists, what would you like to hear God say when you arrive at the Pearly Gates?**
  "You were right; it is as good as you thought it was."

✳ SUHANI JALOTA: Founder, Myna Mahila Foundation

"For the woman who has to use a public toilet in India, it can be torture. Men stand around, count the number of times they use them, and harass them. Some women even take pills that constipate themselves so they can avoid using public toilets."

A native of India and a graduate of Duke University (full disclosure: my alma mater—but I am relatively sure this dynamic young woman was not even born when I attended), Suhani Jalota is a real-world Wonder Woman. In her native country, taboos are real, and menstruation is one of them.

Suhani was profiled in *Glamour* magazine as a part of their "2016 College Women of the Year" series, in which she laid out a picture of the enormous roadblocks between the culture and her Vagipreneurial goal: "(M)enstruation is considered impure, and even saying the word period is taboo…I wanted to chip away at that stigma, but how do you change something people aren't even willing to talk about?"[19] Suhani was awarded the $20,000 grand prize from *Glamour* and invested the money back in the business. More recently, she was named a winner of the British 2017 Queen's Young Leader Award for her work in global women's health. In addition to receiving mentoring and other benefits, she met Queen Elizabeth II (yes, *that* Queen).[20]

Suhani was inspired after doing volunteer work in the slums of India, side-by-side with the women who lived there. She saw women

---

[19] Militare, Jessica. "2016 College Women of the Year: Suhani Jalota." *Glamour*. April 05, 2017. https://www.glamour.com/story/suhani-jalota-2016-college-women-of-the-year.

[20] "Suhani Jalota '16 Named 2017 Queen's Young Leader Award Winner." January 30, 2017. https://econ.duke.edu/news/suhani-jalota-16-named-2017-queens-young-leader-award-winner.

using leaves, old cloths, and rags to manage their periods because sanitary products were either beyond their means or completely unavailable. That crystallized a vision in her mind: If she changed the conversation to economic and individual empowerment rather than focusing on the physiological aspects of periods, she could empower women to beome entrepreneurs by employing them to produce and sell menstrual pads while simultaneously giving them purpose and confidence.

"I was working in the slums of Mumbai as a young teenager for six years on a separate public sanitation project, interviewing women about using public toilets," Suhani says. "That issue, unfortunately, is much larger and more difficult to solve at this time, because it reflects the patriarchal nature of Indian society. You see, there simply aren't enough toilets. And it was eye-opening for me. For the woman who has to use a public toilet in India, it can be torture. Men stand around, count the number of times the women use them, and harass them. Some women even take pills that constipate themselves so they can avoid using public toilets. That whole project opened my eyes to enormous systemic problems in India and made me want to do something that could improve the lives of women who had to live under those conditions."

Fortunately for Suhani and the women she had interviewed, she lived near enough to the Mumbai slums that she didn't lose track of her interview subjects and continued to visit them. She took the time to learn about their lives, gaining a broader perspective of some of the problems she might be able to address once she got to college. With this vision and experience in mind, Suhani founded the Myna Mahila Foundation in June 2015 (mynas are chatty birds; *mahila* means "woman" in the Hindi language).

She decided to work with women on better solutions for managing their periods because she saw women reusing old cloth pieces, washed in water (which of course does not disinfect), dried in dark, hidden places, which compounds the potential for bacterial growth. While reused rags are an obvious health hazard, it has been difficult trying to promote the use of pads over rags.

The cultural differences between India and the West continue to confound people unfamiliar with India. Suhani still receives a lot of questions about her nonprofit's sanitary pad business from people who think they have better ideas without a good understanding of the practical and societal constraints under which she and her staff labor.

"The oddest questions we have been asked are about other forms of sanitary period management," Suhani says, bemused. "'Why aren't you using tampons and diva cups?' Well, for one thing, trying to convince unmarried women in the slums to use internal products would be an uphill battle. Virginity is prized in India, and the perception remains that anything inserted into the body could affect the integrity of the hymen, which rightly or wrongly is still connected to a woman's virginity. We simply cannot tackle something like that enormous cultural shift, especially not at this nascent stage. We currently have a staff of eighteen women and 1,200 loyal clients, but changing the culture is well beyond our scope."

There are also more widespread hygienic issues that make "simple" solutions like diva cups, which are plausible in the West, completely impractical in the slums of India. When there is no access to hot water because there is no electricity, keeping such a device clean becomes a challenge, and what began as a sanitary item becomes a breeding ground for possible infection. Pads are much cleaner and safer. Even the disposal of the new pads presents a logistical problem that Suhani has had to grapple with, because when women have never used pads before and start using them, a safe and reliable way to get rid of the waste is needed. As a result, Suhani is partnering with other organizations to incinerate the pads, which means they must be collected after use and transported for incineration. The end-to-end problem is complex. Myna Mahila has its own factory, and it houses workers for free. They have been permanently relocated from the slums into five rooms in the building, and they manufacture, package, and deliver the sanitary pads. Women sell the product door-to-door on a commission basis at whatever price they believe is fair. This direct-sales approach allows for the kind of one-on-one education and distribution that gently breaks through generations of habit and taboos. Ultimately, Suhani's vision is for girls in India's slums to see opportunities in their lives. Her workers are lifting their families out of poverty through their work manufacturing and selling sanitary pads, after all. "A myna is a talking bird, and I want women talking and having conversations about their futures," says Suhani. "If I were to see these girls come to me after they have worked for Myna Mahila, I would hope they would talk to me about learning, going to school, taking a course, maybe even starting a company. It's difficult with all the constraints in India, but talking about their bodies is the first step toward getting them to talk about their futures." Myna Mahila was selected as one of the charities that Prince Harry and Megan Markle wanted donations sent to in lieu of gifts for their wedding. And Suhani was invited to the royal wedding.

THE QUESTIONS

Suhani Jalota, Founder, Myna Mahila Foundation

- **What is your favorite word?**
  Woman.

- **What is your least favorite word?**
  Ugly. It shouldn't be used.

- **What turns you on creatively, spiritually, or emotionally?**
  Stories about people's lives.

- **What turns you off creatively, spiritually, or emotionally?**
  When older men are very sure about their opinions about things and believe they are facts: a strong, patriarchal mindset.

- **What sound or noise do you love?**
  Slow, romantic music.

- **What sound or noise do you hate?**
  The hiss a snake makes.

- **What is your favorite curse word?**
  Dumbo (I'm not a big curser).

- **What profession other than your own would you like to attempt?**
  I would love to be a politician; it's a great way to create change.

- **What profession would you not like to do?**
  A financial analyst who sits at a desk and crunches numbers.

- **If Heaven exists, what would you like to hear God say when you arrive at the Pearly Gates?**
  "You have made me proud!"

✳ Jordana Kier: Cofounder, LOLA Tampons

---

*"We were actually asked during fundraising
meetings if different size tampons correspond to
different sizes of vaginas!"*

In America, the FDA will regulate just about anything that goes into the human body. But interestingly enough, when Jordana Kier and her business partner, Alexandra Friedman, started to do preliminary research into the tampon industry, they couldn't figure out what exactly any of them were made of.

Labels on boxes in drugstores were decidedly iffy. "This product *may* contain cotton, rayon, *and/or* polyester." Well, does it? Doesn't it? Which, exactly? And in which amounts? This ambiguity in labeling struck Jordana as odd because, as it turns out, the FDA regulates tampons as a medical device, and yet it does not require tampon manufacturers to disclose exactly what they are made of. Women who choose to use tampons can live with these items inside their bodies for up to one-third of their active reproductive days; it seemed unbelievable to Jordana that women aren't allowed to know exactly what they are inserting into their vaginas.

Although Jordana herself may not remember it, there is a good reason for women to be able to know what's in a tampon. When it comes to "medical devices" worn inside the body, newer and higher tech isn't always better. In 1978, Procter & Gamble introduced a superabsorbent tampon brand, Rely, composed of compressed polyester foam and a substance typically used to thicken foods—carboxymethylcellulose. Due to a perfect storm of design timing and changes in FDA regulations, Rely was protected by a grandfather clause and did not have to produce scientific evidence of its safety before it went to market. *Oops.*[21]

By 1980, medical professionals were flummoxed by a troubling spike in Toxic Shock Syndrome (TSS)—essentially an overwhelming systemic *staphylococcus aureus* infection that can be deadly if it isn't caught and treated early enough. What made this outbreak so confusing was that more than 90 percent of sufferers were menstruating women.

Either you remember when this happened or you can probably guess where this story is going.

It turned out the novel composition of Rely tampons created a set of conditions that set the stage for TSS. The new tampons were so superabsorbent, women sometimes left them in much longer than "normal" tampons. And that, combined with pH changes in the vagina during periods, created perfect conditions for staph bacteria overgrowth, which could then enter the bloodstream through any preexisting microabrasions inside the vaginal tract.

Rely was pulled from store shelves in September 1980, but it took many years for women to fully trust tampons again. Today, most women know that it's important to change tampons regularly to avoid the risk of TSS, and every box contains a warning about the syndrome.

But women *still* don't know exactly what's in their tampons.

Enter Lola, which manufactures tampons (and also a line of microthin sanitary pads, among other products) from 100 percent organic cotton along with BPA-free plastic applicators. The company also offers applicator-free tampons for women who prefer to place the product with their own fingers.

---

[21] Vostral, Sharra L. "Rely and Toxic Shock Syndrome: A Technological Health Crisis." *The Yale Journal of Biology and Medicine*. December 2011. Accessed September 24, 2017. https://www.ncbi. nlm.nih.gov/pmc/articles/PMC3238331/.

Oh, and the most distinctive thing about Lola: It's a subscription service. A woman's monthly menstruation management needs are met through a monthly delivery. There's even a "My First Period" kit for girls reaching the age at which they will need that very special box.

"I can't specifically remember a time that was awkward," Jordana says about starting Lola. "Maybe telling my dad about the business, but that's just a matter of feeling momentarily uncomfortable and getting past it. These topics may be initially uncomfortable, but they're incredibly important."

You said it, sister.

Jordana says she and Alex were initially inspired to launch Lola when they were struck by the realization that women approach nearly every other aspect of their health and wellness with more care and attention than they do their reproductive health. Importantly, they see their startup as not just a sanitary products company, but as a part of a movement to help women take ownership of their bodies and their purchasing behavior. But at the same time, she says, "It's interesting; a lot of women don't want to know anything about their periods. They're turned off by it. So, we've taken the building of this company as an opportunity to educate. We were actually asked during fundraising meetings if different size tampons correspond to different sizes of vaginas! So we had to keep a straight face and explain, no, the vagina itself is very elastic; tampon sizes relate to the heaviness or lightness of menstrual flow. That was quite a day."

What she learned along the way was that basic menstrual ignorance wasn't limited to investors, either. She noted in another interview that even a male physician (*yes! A physician! Who presumably attended and graduated from medical school!*) once asked her if women use one tampon per period.[22] (That would be a big, fat no, Doc.)

Jordana was raised in an open, communicative family. She says she could ask her parents anything and didn't shy away from any topics, which gave her the initial confidence to walk into a room full of strangers and talk about reproductive health issues without embarrassment. And she thinks that spirit of openness is now moving into the wider world. "Ten years ago, I wouldn't have been able to build this company. Women's health issues simply weren't talked about so openly. Have you heard about the woman who ran the London Marathon free-bleeding, without any sanitary products at all, to raise awareness about women worldwide who have no access to sanitary products? *Whoa.* She received a lot of criticism, but she was astonishingly brave. And the internet has opened up a lot of other discussions; 'My friend has never had an orgasm' will get tons of clicks and shares today. Women want to talk about their sexual and reproductive health, even if a lot of them are initially shy about it."

Remember the first rule of Fight Club? *You do not talk about Fight Club.* Well, for strong Vagipreneurs, the opposite is true. You *must* talk about it. The kind of openness, transparency, and conversations Lola is starting around women's bodies and their needs is coupled with extreme convenience. Through the subscription model, women might never again need to make an emergency run to the nearest store for supplies when their periods arrive unexpectedly.

It's a story of a well-researched premise, based on consumer desire for as much information about the medical devices women

---

[22] Geddes, Stephanie & Wielopolski, Magdalena. "Jordana Kier and Alexandra Friedman" *Bird.* http://www.wearebird.co/jordana-and-alexandra/.

place inside our bodies as we expect from our food, our medications, and our t-shirts. (Label check: 90 percent cotton, 10 percent spandex. There. *Was that so hard*?)

THE QUESTIONS:

Jordana Kier, Cofounder, Lola

- **What is your favorite word?**
  Yes.

- **What is your least favorite word?**
  No.

- **What turns you on creatively, spiritually, or emotionally?**
  A sense of humor.

- **What turns you off creatively, spiritually, or emotionally?**
  Laziness.

- **What sound or noise do you love?**
  My shower turning on.

- **What sound or noise do you hate?**
  Nails on a chalkboard.

- **What is your favorite curse word?**
  Fuck.

- **What profession other than your own would you like to attempt?**
  Trained musician. I was a pianist and would love to be the drummer for Fleetwood Mac (if Mick Fleetwood ever wanted to take a vacation).

- **What profession would you not like to do?**
  Banker.

- **If Heaven exists, what would you like to hear God say when you arrive at the Pearly Gates?"**
  "I wasn't expecting you yet."

CHAPTER 5

Business Models: Transforming the Women's Health Space through Reimagined Approaches to the Marketplace

want to take a moment here to point out something that became more apparent to me as I interviewed Vagipreneurs. As I categorized businesses and stories and assigned them to chapters within the book, almost every person I interviewed had multiple lessons to impart across multiple categories.

New technology, for example, is also by its very nature creative. New approaches to distribution channels also represent new business models. Creative solutions and technology often require education, and so on. The aspect of each business I chose to focus on was ultimately driven by the subjects covered in each interview and by the unique aspects of each interviewee's experience in the women's health and wellness space. Of course, there was always a degree of category overlap when it came time to decide what I would highlight; most often, my biggest challenge was picking which aspect of each journey to place in the spotlight.

"Business model" is one of those terms that shows up in boardrooms and around conference tables so often, it sometimes loses its meaning. And yet nailing down what, precisely, a business model *is* can be tricky. Like Potter Stewart's famous Supreme Court definition of pornography from the 1964 *Jacobellis v. Ohio* decision, "business model" may be hard to precisely explain, but nearly everybody agrees, "I know it when I see it."

At its most fundamental level, a business model is simply a definition of *how a company will make money*. It may be writing and selling apps, or a subscription service that packages and delivers the ingredients for a night's dinner, or using heightened forms of web security to create interactive health data systems, or any other of an almost limitless combination of products, services, and ways to get products and services into the hands of customers. From my perspective, a new business model is a commitment to take new approaches or new distribution options to solving problems in existing delivery platforms, to identify gaps, and to say, "we can do this better."

In the women's health and wellness space, a few luminaries are actively engaged in redefining how the delivery of products and services can be transformed, reimagined, and re-engineered as money-making enterprises—while importantly (which in and of itself reflects a new model) also doing good in the world. And with good reason. In the past two decades, the number of women-owned businesses has grown at a rate *five times the national average*.[23]

One of the players making waves through her business model is Tracy Warren of Astarte Ventures—a venture capital firm dedicated in its entirety to funding businesses in the women's and children's health sectors.

---

[23] "The 2016 State of Women-Owned Businesses Report Commissioned by American Express OPEN." http://www.womenable.com/content/userfiles/2016_State_of_Women-Owned_Businesses_Executive_Report.pdf.

✳ TRACY WARREN: Founder, Astarte Ventures

"I woke up and thought, why do we keep waiting for
people to be sick? It's very hard to change human behavior.
We need to move from pure treatment to wellness and
prevention, and early intervention. And I realized the
women's health space will have to be driven by consumer
choice and behavior."

Is there any field in business that's more "Boy's Club" than venture capital? My old $100 bill from Zestra pitch meeting days says "no."

Add to that the hue and cry and near-daily media coverage surrounding the dearth of female investors, sexual predators being unmasked across nearly every economic sector, and the significant minority of venture capital (VC) funds that go to women founders.

All of these factors make Astarte Ventures, along with other highly specialized, women-run, women-focused venture capital firms, a game-changer. With a clearly defined focus on investing in companies that target women—who constitute the overwhelming majority of decision-makers in most aspects of health-care—Astarte knows exactly where it wants to be: at the forefront of the next wave of health spending. Astarte funds specialty ventures that offer at least one of three specific things to women between the ages of twenty-five and sixty-five with discretionary income to spend on their own or their children's health and wellness: more control, more capacity for managing health, and/or more convenience.

Tracy Warren, who is a serial entrepreneur and a managing partner of Astarte Ventures, is not the sort of woman one might expect to find in the boardroom of a venture capital firm, which is probably *why* she's in the boardroom of a women-focused VC firm. She grew up in a small, rural Michigan town on ten acres, attending a Lutheran school from kindergarten through high school and says, "My early life was sort of like *Little House on the Prairie.* It was a working- to middle-class upbringing. Everybody in the town worked for General Motors. The school I attended was really a feeder to the ministry, but I knew very early on that was not my destiny. I saw *Working Girl,* the 1980s film, and I knew I needed to go, so I went to New York University, never having even been to the city before. And I was immediately enamored with its diversity, its culture, its pace."

(As a huge fan of *Working Girl,* when I interviewed Tracy I could hear Carly Simon singing in the background at this point as Melanie Griffith playing Tess McGill rides the Staten Island Ferry toward her new life in the big city.) As the first in her family to attend college, all was not smooth sailing for Tracy right out of the gate. In fact, she says, her father—a police officer—almost disowned her when she first left home for New York. "Nobody got me. It was this big, crazy thing. I started working in finance, and I was also working nights at a bar, waitressing, which isn't bad. Customer service is one of the many things you need to learn along the way. But in the finance world, you work insane hours with no weekends off and no vacations. My family thought working for a bank meant being a teller; Mom worked for a utility company from 7:30–4:30 p.m., Monday through Friday, for forty years, and in that kind of job, you don't take work home with you. Plus, all the movies about shady business in high finance like *Wall Street* didn't make things easier. Mom still makes jokes about those."

Then decades later, along came a television show called *Shark Tank,* and finally, Tracy's family began to understand. OK, so maybe raising money isn't *exactly* like it's portrayed in the show, and you don't always get direct access to famous investors, athletes, and businesspeople, but it sure helped Tracy's discussions with her family.

"Now, at last, I can talk about investment strategies and women's health technologies with my family. I can talk with them about our investment portfolio, which includes Madorra, a nonhormonal device that treats vaginal dryness. I can talk about the Naya breast pump, a smart device that not only lets women pump more milk in less time, but also tracks pumping sessions and milk supply like a Fitbit. I can talk with them about an exciting new device, Lully, that cuts down on children's night terrors by up to 80 percent and lets everybody get more healthy sleep. And I can talk to them about Maven, the first women-exclusive online health clinic, built around the convenience of instant access, because women don't have the time to wait weeks for an appointment, or to take a half-day off work when they need to talk to somebody about a health care concern." (The Madorra device Tracy mentioned above is also featured in this book.)

Tracy's children, who are fourteen, eleven, and nine, also love talking about her work and like the children's aspect of Astarte's mission. I have to admit that I am a little bit jealous of Tracy's children's enthusiasm for her work: my now-college-age son, whose mom has been in the vagina business for a *long* time, has asked me on more than one occasion, "For the love of God, can you work on a business—any single business—with a focus that is out of the underwear?"

When I asked Tracy what she wishes she'd known before she started on her journey, she said, "That intelligence and common sense can sometimes be mutually exclusive. I've met some highly educated hedge-fund professionals who can be completely unaware. They're very practical about running, building, and financing a business, but if the numbers look right, they ignore glaring softer signs that can often indicate clear risk factors."

Tracy is no newcomer or stranger to venture capital or the medical space. The catalyst for founding Astarte was fifteen years of completing a fair number of deals on medical issues that Tracy couldn't personally relate to. She did the research, spoke with physicians, leveraged business intelligence, and landed successes in enormous categories, but ultimately realized she was not personally passionate about them. "One day," she says, "I woke up and thought, why do we keep waiting for people to be sick? It's very hard to change human behavior. We need to move from pure treatment to wellness, prevention, and early intervention. And I realized the women's health space will have to be driven by consumer choice and behavior. As women gain greater economic power, women's health care will follow. If I don't have something to do with figuring it out, then someone *else* will figure it out."

That's what Tracy finds frustrating, above all else. "Oh, the inertia in the system is *maddening*," she says, "especially when it comes to women's health. It's still a very misogynistic system. Did you know women still have to suffer through two miscarriages to qualify for a cerclage procedure to treat cervical incompetence or insufficiency? That's insane. And yet, in our system, when things have always been a certain way, the default is to wait for somebody else to make a change, as opposed to making an effort to make waves. So much intellectual horsepower; so few transformational leaders."

Despite her unrelenting drive and laser-like focus, Tracy is not exempt from the same social taboos and pressures that rear their heads at other Vagipreneurs. At one memorable investor dinner, she remembers being asked the kinds of questions one always hears at business events: "What do you do? Where do you work?" Without hesitation or a second thought, she answered. "I work in women's and children's health." The man who had asked assumed her answer meant global health and said so. In her excitement to share the kinds of innovations Astarte funds, Tracy began to clarify: "No, things like a new kind of breast pump, and cures for vaginal dryness, and relief for menopause…"

Without thinking, her dinner companion leveled a cool gaze and said, "I don't think this is appropriate dinner conversation."

Tracy disagrees. And so do I. What isn't appropriate? Talking about businesses that are good for the world *and* make money?

Tracy is on a mission to do both.

THE QUESTIONS

Tracy Warren, Astarte Ventures

- **What is your favorite word?**
  Kaleidoscope.

- **What is your least favorite word?**
  Like.

- **What turns you on creatively, spiritually, or emotionally?**
  Two or more distinct positions where you want to sort everything out, with no one right answer.

- **What turns you off creatively, spiritually, or emotionally?**
  Judgmental people and biases.

- **What sound or noise do you love?**
  My kids laughing.

- **What sound or noise do you hate?**
  Barking dogs.
- **What is your favorite curse word?**
  Fuck.
- **What profession other than your own would you like to attempt?**
  CIA agent.
- **What profession would you not like to do?**
  Politician.
- **If Heaven exists, what would you like to hear God say when you arrive at the Pearly Gates?**
  Either "Nice job," or "I didn't expect to see you."

✳ CINDY GALLOP: Founder, Make Love Not Porn

"The same young people who would never in a million years actually think about donning home-stitched superhero capes and leaping from bridges or buildings are, without thinking critically, emulating the same kinds of over-the-top, unrealistic behaviors when they see them in pornography, assuming this is 'how it's done.'"

So.

Would you rent a streaming video of your friends or neighbors having sex?

I am asking a serious question. That's exactly what the business model of makelovenotporn.tv is all about.

Founder Cindy Gallop, a fearless and outspoken Brit who landed on the world stage with a thunderous *kaboom* in 2009 with a four-minute TED Talk, calls it "social sex." She figures if we are willing to share photos and videos of every other aspect of our lives, there will probably come a day when more people will be comfortable producing and sharing (more) real-life, real-world, uncontrived, healthy, happy, nonpornographic sex.[24]

As it turns out, she's on to something pretty big. The people who share their homemade creations—she calls them MakeLoveNotPornStars—aren't shy about sharing. And I have to admit that any time I speak to Cindy or hear her speak, I think of Susan Sarandon's Thelma in *Thelma and Louise*: "I don't ever remember feelin' this awake."

"There wasn't a particular moment when I decided to do this," Cindy says. "MakeLoveNotPorn was a complete and utter accident. Every year, TED invites members of the audience to do what Chris Anderson, the owner of TED, calls 'palate cleansers'—a short talk between the long sessions. In 2009, when he put out a call for palate cleansers, I proposed one, as I was working on MakeLoveNotPorn at the time and it was still very early going. I did it partially as a joke, because I didn't think it would be accepted.

"But Chris got back to me immediately. He told me, 'This is a serious issue, and I want you to do this, but we just need to talk about it first.' I explained that the site would consist only of words and design; Porn World versus Real World, with no graphic or sexually explicit content at all. And then, of course, the world responded, and I felt a huge responsibility to take it forward."

---

[24] Gallop, Cindy. "Make Love, Not Porn | Cindy Gallop." *YouTube*, TedTalks, 2 Dec. 2009, www.youtube.com/watch?v=FV8n_E_6Tpc&feature=youtube.

The serious issue Cindy talked about was this: An entire generation raised on readily accessible internet pornography has received its education about human sexuality from hardcore porn. Young people—men *and* women—have no frame of reference about what is "normal" versus what is exaggerated, unrealistic, overemphasized, choreographed, or faked for the camera. "The same young people who would never in a million years actually think about donning home-stitched superhero capes and leaping from bridges or buildings are, without thinking critically, emulating the same kinds of over-the-top, unrealistic behaviors when they see them in pornography, assuming this is 'how it's done,'" Cindy says.

Cindy came to this realization through personal experience. "I started dating younger men nine or ten years ago," she says, "and I began realizing that I was experiencing what happens when two things converge: when today's total freedom of access to hardcore pornography online meets our society's equally total reluctance to talk openly and honestly about sex. When that happens, porn becomes sex education by default—not in a good way. That was the basis of my four minutes on the TED stage, and the world responded. I realized I'd uncovered a huge global social issue, and I took MakeLoveNotPorn forward by turning it into a business that does good and makes money simultaneously—MakeLoveNotPorn. tv, the world's first and only social sex video-sharing platform that welcomes and curates user-generated videos celebrating real-world sex. We're not porn, and we're not amateur. We're building a whole new category on the internet that's never previously existed: social sex. Our competition isn't porn—it's Facebook and YouTube, or rather, it would be if Facebook and YouTube allowed social sexual self-expression, which they don't. At MakeLoveNotPorn, we call ourselves the 'Social Sex Revolution.' The revolutionary part isn't the sex—it's the social."

Lest anybody think Cindy is anti-sex or anti-porn, makelovenotporn.tv's tagline puts that myth to bed (so to speak) with a big, splashy tagline one absolutely cannot miss: "Pro-sex. Pro-porn. Pro-knowing the difference." That's the key to everything.

"Because we don't talk about sex, it's an area of rampant insecurity around the world," Cindy says. "We all get vulnerable when we are naked. It's therefore bizarrely difficult to talk about sex with the person you are actually having it with *while* you are actually having it. You worry that if you are commenting on the act at all, you will potentially hurt your partner's feelings, derail the encounter, possibly even the relationship. And that's incredibly frustrating. Sad. Tragic, really. Everybody wants to be good in bed, yet no one knows exactly what that means. So, you'll seize on cues from anywhere you can. If the only cues you've ever seen are in porn, because your parents didn't talk to you about sex and your school didn't teach you and your friends don't talk about it, those are the only cues you'll take, to not-very-good effect."

As a businesswoman, Cindy observes that pornography is like any other industry. It has gotten so big that it's gotten conventional, with its own rules and clichés. The advent of free porn online has destroyed its old-world-order business model. "The explosive growth of extreme, violent porn isn't driven by evil, twisted, malicious forces," Cindy says. "Very prosaically, it's driven by a bunch of guys scared shitless because they're not making as much money anymore, doing what bunches of guys scared shitless when they're not making money in *any* industry do—playing it safe. So, they look around, and they think, 'What can I do that's new?' In an industry that has no idea how to invent its own future, the only way to innovate is, well, *more holes*. More *extreme performances*. They think that's what the consumer wants.

"The porn industry is ripe for innovation and disruption. When it comes to porn, people watch what they are given. And in a male-dominated industry, that means watching things produced and directed predominantly through the male lens. The day we have a porn industry that is equally led and driven by women as much as men, which therefore targets as much of its output at women as at men, and which makes as much of its money from women as from men? That will be the day we have porn and a porn industry that looks completely different: more innovative, more disruptive, more creative, and *far* more lucrative. A better, healthier industry overall. The same is true of every other industry: movies, television, advertising."

Cindy is just getting warmed up.

"The reason 'amateur' is the biggest growth sector in porn has nothing to do with porn. It has everything to do with the fact that everybody wants to know what everybody else is *really* doing in bed, and *nobody knows*. At last, with MakeLoveNotPorn's social sex, we're showing them. Every single day for the past nine years, since the site launched, I have received emails. *Thousands* of emails. From young people. Old people. Men and women. Straight and gay. People pour their hearts out because of what they've seen on *MakeLoveNotPorn*, about their sex lives and other areas as well. So, we *are* starting important conversations. And the answer *isn't* to block or advocate for the end of porn. We all watch porn. We just don't talk about it. When you force an entire industry into the shadows, you make it easier for bad things to happen, and you make it a lot more difficult for good things to happen. We're trying to open up a dialogue about real sex. The issue isn't porn; it's our complete failure to talk openly and honestly about sex. I started a social sex platform to change that, and I encourage other entrepreneurs to disrupt the 'adult' world as well. I like to repurpose a quote from Wayne LaPierre, of the National Rifle Association: *The only thing that stops a bad guy with a business is a good guy with a better business.*"

Like other Vagipreneurs, Cindy has hit roadblock after roadblock in her journey.

"I fight a huge battle every single day to build this business," she says. "Every piece of business infrastructure any other startup can take for granted, we can't access. We cannot find funding. We cannot get technical services. We cannot find payment services willing to work with us. We cannot get banks to service our accounts. Three words have thrown up barriers at every turn: **No Adult Content**."

That doesn't mean she'll give up anytime soon. In fact, like most of the Vagipreneurs I interviewed, Cindy is a woman on a mission. Hers is to make real-world sex socially acceptable to talk about—and ultimately, just as socially shareable and profitable for those who share it. In the process, she has literally become a social media phenom. She is aware of the irony that she and her efforts are well-known, but still not well-funded. (In fact, recently, after seeing Cindy struggle and fail for three years to raise the funding MakeLoveNotPorn so badly needed, and having *himself* pitched other investors and failing, Cindy's original angel investor volunteered to complete an entire funding round of $2 million himself.)

At Make Love Not Porn, the everyday people who create and upload #realworldsex content—MakeLoveNotPornStars—receive 50 percent of the revenues when people rent their videos. Cindy intentionally designed her revenue-sharing business model this way—an upending of the business model of traditional porn, in which performers are paid once, and that's that. "I believe everybody should realize the financial value of what they create," says Cindy, whose background is a stellar career in advertising and theater. "When you create something that gives others pleasure, well…the more pleasure you give to more people, the more money you should make. In porn, whether you are a newbie or a star, you get paid by the scene, and that starts at a few hundred dollars and maxes out at $1,000 to $2,000 a day. No matter how many millions of times those scenes are viewed, the stars make no additional money. I designed MakeLoveNotPorn around what I believe is the business model of the future: Shared Values + Shared Action = Shared Profit, both financial and social. Our MakeLoveNotPornStars' earning potential is uncapped."

She continues.

"We spent years concepting and designing MakeLoveNotPorn. tv, because we knew that if we were going to invite people to do something they've never done before—socially share their real-world sex—we had to think through every ramification to create a safe and trustworthy space. It's not possible to complete our submissions process unless your video is fully consensual and legal—we require two forms of visual ID for every participant. We curate all of the content personally, watching every video submitted from beginning to end to make sure it's real. Then we Skype with our MakeLoveNotPorn stars to build a relationship with them. As a MakeLoveNotPornStar, you can choose your own comfort level. For instance, if you are concerned about being recognized, it's fine to be anonymous; you can wear a mask or keep your face out of frame. Your videos are only viewable on the platform via streaming, not download, and the second you change your mind, those videos are gone. It's both empowering and frustrating building this brand-new platform, because we need funding to scale, and I cannot find investors. The business case is crystal clear; our biggest obstacle, raising funding, is simply the social dynamic I call 'fear of what other people will think.' And by the way, fear of what other people will think is the most paralyzing dynamic in business and in life. You will never own the future if you care what other people think."

Cindy isn't going to stop talking about social sex. She's building the MakeLoveNotPorn community offline as well as online with gatherings in the real world as well, where MakeLoveNotPornStars come together to have a friendly drink, network, get to know each other, and connect. It's a natural extension of the company's mission to take the very dynamic that exists in social media and apply it to socializing, normalizing, destigmatizing, and sharing sex—the Social Sex Revolution.

THE QUESTIONS

Cindy Gallop, MakeLoveNotPorn.tv

- **What is your favorite word?**
  Women.

- **What is your least favorite word?**
  Stop.

- **What turns you on creatively, spiritually, or emotionally?**
  Anybody who doesn't care what anyone else thinks.

- **What turns you off creatively, spiritually, or emotionally?**
  Anybody who cares too much what other people think.

- **What sound or noise do you love?**
  The sound of ice in a cocktail shaker shaking up a martini.

- **What sound or noise do you hate?**
  Silence when someone should be speaking up.

- **What is your favorite curse word?**
  Fuck.

- **What profession other than your own would you like to attempt?**
  I wouldn't. I only want to do what I'm doing right now—sex tech entrepreneur.

- **What profession would you not like to do?**
  Any profession where you have to worry about what other people think.

- **If Heaven exists, what would you like to hear God say when you arrive at the Pearly Gates?**
  "You can drink as many martinis and have as much sex with as many younger men as you want."

✳ POLLY RODRIGUEZ: Founder and CEO, Unbound, and Cofounder, Women of Sex Tech

"Who wants to go through the story of her cancer, treatment, loss of fertility and her libido five times a day? I don't want to do this every day—I have to. When things get difficult, I remind myself that little by little, story by story, repetition by repetition, it's changing things."

"It's the number one question I get—what in the world motivated you to start doing this?" says Polly Rodriguez, a wholeheartedly engaged thirty-year-old who's as much an evangelist and prophet of Vagipreneurship as she is a fiercely committed founder and executive of her own women's-sexuality-related company.

"Honestly, what led me to create Unbound was a mix of market opportunity and personal pain. I thought I knew what I was getting into. I'd been a high-level business consultant straight out of college, helping huge corporations maximize profits and cut costs. I'd worked on strategy. All those things. But when it came to launching a company dedicated to sexual pleasure? *I had no idea.* People tried to warn me it was going to be extremely challenging to start up a business in this space. I initially waved it off; *how hard could it be?* Well, it's been so hard, it's blown me away. *That's* how hard it's been."

The personal pain Polly alludes to is the kind that nobody her age (or any age, for that matter) should, in a fair world, be intimately familiar with. At age twenty-one, after three years of troubling symptoms had been minimized and misdiagnosed, she was diagnosed with stage IIIC colorectal cancer—the last treatable stage before the disease is officially deemed terminal. Before surgery, she underwent radiation therapy to shrink the size of the tumor. But that treatment also had a significant, permanent side effect, sending Polly into premature menopause because the radiation also affected her ovaries.

The thing that struck Polly most, once she'd come out the other side? "My doctors didn't even think this was a side effect of radiation worth mentioning in plain, everyday language. They brought up the possibility of harvesting my eggs to address my loss of fertility, but nothing about libido or other effects of sudden radiation-related menopause on sexual function. If you're a man and you're undergoing surgery or radiation for cancer, and it's going to affect your sexual function, those discussions *happen*. Me? I had to find out what to expect by Googling, essentially."

During those dark times, her family was always there for her. Especially her father, himself a cancer survivor who taught her valuable lessons about beating odds that seem insurmountable—lessons she would later carry with her beyond cancer treatment and into the boardroom.

"My dad is also an entrepreneur—although he came to it late in life, once he saw me do it," Polly laughs. "Before that, he spent most of his career in real estate. He's the son of a Spanish immigrant. I'm a lot like my father in terms of temperament. He *lives* to laugh. He takes *nothing* too seriously. When he was going through cancer himself, at the time, in his twenties, there was really nothing you could do about the form he had—it was jaw cancer, and all they could do was surgically remove his entire jawbone and replace it with metal. So that's exactly what they did. For eighteen months, when I was a child, my dad's mouth was wired shut. I remember right after I was diagnosed, I was online one night, late, researching my own cancer, and Dad came into the room. He found me in a puddle of tears: "Oh my God, Dad, I'm reading all these people's stories and they've all got the same kind of cancer I do, and they all say they're going to die.

"Dad walked up to the computer, shut it off, and said, 'If I *ever* catch you reading something like that again, I will throw that computer away.' I was taken aback, but it startled me. It brought me up short. I asked, 'Wait, why?'

"And that's when he told me, 'Because that's a very dark place for you to go. When I was diagnosed when you were little, it was long before the internet, so I went to the university medical library and started looking up survival statistics. Then I went to my own doctor and said, "Doc, I checked it out, and these books say I only have a single-digit chance to beat this thing." My doctor told me to *stop it*. He said *none of those statistics mean anything*. He told me it's *all* a matter of mental toughness. To think about nothing but how I was going to beat my cancer. To think about how I was going to be *fine*. So that's what I did.'"

Polly pauses for only a few seconds before saying, "Ever since then, I've worked hard to approach my entire life with that same mentality: Focus on and believe in the things you want. I've never read *The Secret*, but from what I've heard, I think it's essentially the same approach. And in that one dark evening, my Dad changed the way I think about the whole world as I was facing my cancer. Once you've faced that, you can pretty much face anything."

Almost makes building a business sound simple in comparison.

What are some of the other challenges Polly has faced? The usual.

"People I've approached during the course of starting up Unbound don't even want to have a conversation about sexual pleasure," Polly says, clearly exasperated. "I think that's what has surprised me most about this endeavor so far. I'm obviously very used to hearing the word 'no,' as a young woman in the business world just getting started. You expect to hear 'no.' But in this particular space, it's especially stark. People don't want to discuss sexual products or issues." That's where Polly's unique life experiences created an opening that few people operating in the space have been able to find—a distinct and credible narrative, born of a personal journey joined with airtight business acumen.

Unbound seeks to do more than just sell sexual aids, lubricants, lingerie, and jewelry through a subscription service. It's a full project dedicated to transparency about sexuality, sexual pleasure, and sex-positivity. Unbound lives up to its name with an onsite magazine full of product reviews, stories, interviews, and open discussions, as well as product descriptions that fully disclose each item's materials, manufacturer, geographic source, and purpose. The site, the box, and the experience of shopping or browsing onsite are not bound by conventional notions of shame or discomfort. Unbound is in the business of demolishing the taboos and boundaries that have historically surrounded discussions of sex and women's sexual pleasure. And the company is working on changing those discussions while it delivers products women want through a direct-to-consumer business model that bypasses the dimly lit, sketchy-neighborhood, brick-and-mortar sex-toy shops that once catered primarily to men.

One of Polly's most challenging experiences growing the company began with the inspiration to craft a more personal fundraising pitch.

"When I first started pitching, I was not at all comfortable," Polly remembers. "And certainly, talking about my health journey hadn't occurred to me within the context of pitching for Unbound. But I was raised in a family of extraordinary women. My aunt is a quadriplegic. When I was first starting Unbound, partly because of my aunt, and through introductions from another female entrepreneur, I'd become involved in a group called Diversability, which is an advocacy group for people living with various forms of disability. The group highlights the ways in which disabilities empower those who live with them, making us uniquely strong and resilient. It was at that group that I was encouraged to first get up and tell my *own* story. Initially, I was reluctant to even share. I remember thinking, *how can I possibly stand up and share a cancer-and-early-menopause story in front of people living with cerebral palsy or quadriplegia? That just seems wrong.* But they encouraged me. 'This is what the group is *for*.' So I did it. I told my own story for the very first time to a room full of people, and I explained everything I'd gone through, everything that had changed so suddenly for me when all of my contemporaries were still casually dating, and suddenly I was facing the loss of my fertility and a crashing libido. And I sobbed. The whole way through.

"Afterwards, my entrepreneur mentor pulled me aside and said, '*That* is the story you need to use to pitch investors.' She was right. *That* is why I am so passionate about female health and sexuality. My experience was the catalyst and my *raison d'etre* for Unbound.

"Still, initially hearing that I should bring that experience into venture capital boardrooms terrified me. Because honestly, simply pitching my *company* terrified me. Now I was hearing I should also lay out the most intimate details about my *personal* health journey as well. That's a lot of vulnerability to ask from a founder in a single meeting with strangers. But eventually I came around, and now I actually embrace it—reluctantly at times, but I embrace it. I think vulnerability gave me credibility in investors' eyes. Because in this category, in this industry, it's too easy to write off both people and companies due to preconceived notions about why people choose to go into it. My extremely personal narrative worked against that grain and helped me to establish a form of respectability that set me far apart."

The intertwined narratives of Polly's personal cancer journey and the founding of Unbound cut both ways, though, and that can extract a psychic and emotional price that other entrepreneurs aren't asked to pay.

Polly was profiled in *Teen* Vogue in 2015 in a story about her cancer journey. "Because my personal story went public so quickly, I don't have the luxury of separating my personal life and my professional life," Polly says. "Sometimes, I do have to admit, it can be an emotional drain. Who wants to go through the story of her cancer, treatment, loss of fertility, and libido *five times a day?* I don't *want* to do this every day—I *have to.* But when things get difficult, I remind myself that little by little, story by story, repetition by repetition, it's changing things. It's opening the discussion up, month by month, year by year. And I'm also doing it for the sake of my business. I just closed $2.8 million in funding for Unbound, which is pretty amazing for a female sexual health business that isn't pharmaceutical—especially one that's solely dedicated to female pleasure. So, I am incredibly proud of that. Still, it takes its toll." Polly rejuvenates, refreshes, and draws strength from those strong women in her family, including her social worker mother who worked her entire life, except the two years when Polly and her sister (sixteen months her junior) were first born. While other family members may have initially joked about Polly's sex toy subscription box business idea or asked a rapid-fire succession of sincere questions about it, she says her mother was mostly concerned about what would happen if it didn't work out.

"They were not ridiculous questions. 'Will you ever be able to get another job again? You always wanted to go into politics. Could that happen after you've worked in this industry?'"

The women in Polly's family have *always* been leaders. Her maternal grandmother, Clara Jane, was a landscape architect and a trailblazer in her own right—a member of one of the first graduating classes of the University of Florida. Polly remembers Clara Jane as a true Southern spitfire—a successful business owner, a woman who had her own money and used it to buy anything she wanted for herself (in an era when women didn't do that), and an "insanely liberal Democrat in the Deep South." On the other side of the family, her father's mother owned an antique dealership and Polly says she, too, was always working. "It's funny," she remembers, "because as my grandfathers both got older, they seemed to want to retire and 'enjoy life.' Not my grandmothers. For them, working *was* enjoying life. And now my mom is carrying on the family tradition. She's sixty-five? Sixty-six? And she doesn't want to retire. 'Why would I want to retire? I'd lose my mind!'

"So, the women in my family have role-modeled, for me, what work can be—the sense of purpose it can provide. That, coupled with surviving cancer at such an early age, knowing I couldn't have my own children, gaining that perspective—it all freed me up from societal expectations and the pressure to find somebody, settle down, have kids on the usual timetables in the usual way. If I do decide to have children, I'll adopt them. I don't have the same time constraints as my peers. In a way, it goes back to some of the messages I absorbed in Diversability—the course of my life will be different than other people's lives, but it will be different in ways that are strong, resilient, original, and purposeful."

One of Polly's purposeful endeavors is to bring together other strong women working in Vagipreneurial enterprises through Women of Sex Tech (womenofsextech.com), a consortium of female entrepreneurs working in the sex tech industry, including the arts, education, and business. The group is a supportive network and community for women who have affirmatively chosen to swim upstream in the emerging white space of women's sexual health and wellness. Cofounded by Polly and Lidia Bonilla in 2015, some of the group's members include familiar names like Cindy Gallop of MakeLoveNotPorn and others whose stories are also told here, including Alex Fine of Dame Products and Meika Hollender of Sustain.

Polly is a woman who seems destined to blaze a new path, no matter what she does in life. Watch her go!

THE QUESTIONS

Polly Rodriguez, Unbound

- **What is your favorite word?**
  Milagro, *which means miracle in Spanish.*

- **What is your least favorite word?**
  Any words that are derogatory to people.

- **What turns you on creatively, spiritually, or emotionally?**
  Other women who choose a path that is nontraditional.

- **What turns you off creatively, spiritually, or emotionally?**
  Pessimism.

- **What sound or noise do you love?**
  A cackle-laugh that is infectious.

- **What sound or noise do you hate?**
  People honking on car horns when you're walking.

- **What is your favorite curse word?**
  Shit.

- **What profession other than your own would you like to attempt?**
  Politician—We need to raise the bar. We absolutely need

more women and smart, young people in politics. Young people are too apathetic about politics, and we need smart young people to try to shape the rules.

- **What profession would you not like to do?**
  Accounting. It's so boring.

- **If Heaven exists, what would you like to hear God say when you arrive at the Pearly Gates?**
  "Don't worry. There'll be a sequel."

CHAPTER 6

Creative Solutions:
Finding Better Products for Existing Problems

ooking at a problem; applying problem-solving skills; thinking outside the box (or the crate, or the bubble wrap, or the envelope, or the custom-molded polymer case); coming up with innovative solutions nobody else has come up with before; or configuring and offering them in ways nobody else has to bring a new solution to market. That's the heart of creativity. It can manifest itself in ways that are low-tech, high-tech, and everything in between.

The Vagipreneurs who are bringing novel approaches to women's health and wellness through creative solutions all have, by definition, birthed and nurtured something meaningfully different or new and brought it to the marketplace. They're not just products or services; these people bring commercial enterprises into the world with a critical *woman's perspective on women's health.*

It may seem deceptively intuitive to say that applying a woman's eye to health and wellness issues is an exercise in creativity, but bear with me as we take a look at one of the most successful companies on the face of the planet today and a relatively notorious oversight: Apple. As recently as 2014, when Apple initially released its health kit tracking app, the app was touted in marketing copy as a way for users to look at "your *whole* health picture" (emphasis added)—except for a single astounding oversight.

Periods and reproductive health.

Half of the users of the Health Kit could literally never expect to see their "whole health picture" in Health Kit because there was no way to input information on period dates, let alone more granular female reproductive data such as ovulation tracking, cervical mucus, or fine gradations in body temperature for women who were trying to conceive. It wasn't that the app was incapable of determining whether users were male or female—setup required that data. Women's reproductive health was simply *not there*. After plenty of user feedback and expressions of dismay in the tech press, it took nearly a year for Apple to fill that gap in the app, with a full upgrade released in an iOS update in 2015.[25]

Nobody is entirely certain whether there were women around the table when Health Kit was being built and tested, but its original woman-shaped black hole at launch represented a spectacular failure of awareness of the marketplace. I am not even sure how creative you need to be to think about women's health, given that—as we have mentioned on many an occasion—we constitute roughly 50 percent of the marketplace. But the absence of period tracking rendered Apple's app, likely without malice or any desire to be inconsiderate, a product that was targeted, by default, to men. From a business perspective, it represented a big missed opportunity.

Contrast this with the creative explosion taking place in the smart wearables market today. For both the young, active demographic and for women who are concerned about aging safely *and* gracefully, the days of ugly-but-functional wrist-worn devices have given way to newer, more aesthetically pleasing form factors that look

---

[25] Alba, Davey. "Finally, You'll Be Able to Track Your Period in IOS." *Wired.* September 09, 2015. https://www.wired.com/2015/09/finally-youll-able-track-period-ios/.

like jewelry. In fact, they are being marketed and sold as "smart jewelry," not fitness trackers per se, and they sync with Android and iPhone operating systems just like the first-generation versions of such devices. Outfitted with essentially the same GPS tracking, step counters, and sleep trackers as traditional fitness wearables, but also including period tracking as well as notifications, these new offerings can be worn as necklaces, bracelets, or brooches, and nobody would ever be the wiser about their actual function in the event the wearer didn't want to share.

For older users, engineering is solving another problem. With the addition of fall-detecting accelerometers, you get WiseWear, designed by ninety-five-year-old New York fashion icon Iris Apfel, offering mature women what they truly want: high style in a luxurious form as well as full functionality. Because, yes, women want to be stylish as well as healthy, fit, and safe. Seriously—we don't want to wear something that looks like a small tire around our wrists all day, every day, or a garage door opener around our necks, ruining every decent outfit. This line of wearables is sold, not at sporting goods stores or through infomercials that groan, "Help; I've fallen and I can't get up," but at high-end retailers like Nordstrom, Saks Fifth Avenue, and online for prices that *begin* at $295, proving yet another point; creativity *pays*. When women design products for women, creativity is part of the package.

The leaders of each of the businesses profiled in this chapter made a purposeful decision to jettison the male perspectives, constraints, and barriers that weren't serving their target customers—namely, women. Once they moved women to the center of the conversation and problem they were trying to solve, they unleashed creative forces that drove them forward against strong headwinds. Sure, it helps that many of these founders are potential buyers/users of their solutions, but the opportunities are far greater than the individual.

✳ COLETTE COURTION: CEO and Cofounder, Joylux, Inc.

"My career has been spent helping women tone and tighten. Girlfriends are peeing their pants, losing connection with their partner, and most importantly, losing their confidence. Can we use this technology to tighten, tone, and restore the pelvic floor?"

Colette Courtion, like so many of the women I interviewed for this book, has a high-powered and fascinating professional background. From PepsiCo to Starbucks to medical device manufacturers, she cut her teeth in a variety of industries known for fierce competition and high levels of stress. As the CEO and founder of Joylux, she combined her expertise in medical devices, beauty, and technology to take a highly creative approach to helping the one-in-three women who experience some kind of issue with their pelvic floor. Decreased vaginal tissue and muscular function are a result of damage to the vagina at a nerve, muscle, cellular, or tissue level, caused primarily by childbirth, obesity, or aging. The loss of pelvic floor muscle tone can cause loss of sensation or painful sex as well as urinary incontinence—none of which sound (or are) particularly appealing.

Joylux's first device to treat pelvic floor issues, vSculpt, is currently available in Canada and the United Kingdom, with availability in the United States currently pending as of this book's writing. vSculpt uses LED technology, gentle heat, and sonic vibration to rebuild collagen and strengthen the pelvic floor muscles and help produce more natural lubrication within the vagina, leading to more comfortable sex, improved continence, and better sexual health. Now *that* is a set of benefits that many women can get behind. Lots of women of different ages and life stages.

I asked Colette what her most embarrassing moment as a new entrepreneur in this space was, and she was unfazed. "My feeling is, you must fully embrace the subject of women's sexual health as if it is no different than any other project," she said. "When you're pitching a group of investors, it's usually a group of twenty men over fifty who are not used to discussing these issues. So, when I was looking around the room during my pitches and I could see these men were uncomfortable, I addressed it head-on. 'Hey, men have erectile dysfunction. That's fairly common. There are ads all over television. Well, pelvic floor dysfunction is what women have, and it's time we have a voice, just like you men have.' They honestly didn't believe that this affected their daughters or their wives. It all goes back to a lack of frank, honest dialogue in the bedroom, because whether a man has good sexual response is obvious, and too often, men don't focus on what a woman is getting—or not getting—out of intimate moments."

Colette says the catalyst for launching the company was a moment that came about as if the planets themselves had come into alignment. A combination of technologies she had experience in coalesced. In the beauty and medical/aesthetic technology industry, laser/light therapy helps women rejuvenate their skin, and she had started a successful chain of skin care clinics to help women feel young again. Then when she began thinking about becoming a mom, she started to talk to friends and heard a consistent complaint: "What a lot of women said, honestly, is that you pee your pants." Because vaginal birth or the weight of carrying a baby weakens core muscles and pelvic floor muscles, incontinence after childbirth is common when women laugh or exercise. Colette says she'd had no idea about this phenomenon before those early discussions with her girlfriends. Then she started talking to friends going through menopause only to hear about similar issues. Sex and intimacy are still important to women at this stage in life, obviously, but because of hormonal changes (and many other reasons), the vagina changes. Lubrication levels typically fall. Pelvic floor muscles start to lose tone. Vaginal walls thin. It turns out that women need a solution to this vexing problem across many life stages. Understanding the complexity of a woman's life through different stages—and finding a common solution—is both good thinking and good business.

Colette approached a company that was already interested in using light therapy in conjunction with an aesthetically pleasing, at-home vaginal product, based on trials of light therapy currently being used in Africa by women who don't want to transmit the AIDS virus to their babies. "And that was my light-bulb moment," she says. "I thought, wait a minute. My career has been spent helping women tone and tighten, and my girlfriends are peeing their pants, losing connection with their partners, and most importantly, losing confidence. Can we use this technology to tighten, tone and restore?" This company's leadership said, "Yes, we can."

At this point, physician office-based laser treatments for vaginal rejuvenation were already emerging in the marketplace, but Colette believed most women wanted a home-based solution that was more convenient, private, and affordable. It was 2012, and she noticed that women were beginning to talk about the issue on social media. When she saw vaginas mentioned on a *Real Housewives*-type show, she understood the iron was hot and it was time to strike, so to speak.

"I realized then that in business, timing is everything, and now was our time," Colette says.

Today Colette's son is a toddler, and she can personally relate to those things she heard from her girlfriends when she was gathering informal intelligence on her business concept. As an older mom, she gets it—your body takes longer to bounce back. She says the most frustrating thing about building the business has been the lack of conversation about women's health issues. "It wasn't until we had clinical studies with real medical results and data that the humor dynamic finally dialed down a bit. Men immediately turn to humor to lessen their discomfort; women naturally want to concentrate on the benefits. This device isn't simply a joystick with lights. We've seen results. An independent study showed that 90 percent of users had reduced bladder leakage, with 55 percent of women reporting it was eliminated altogether. Eighty-two percent strengthened their pelvic floor muscles. Eighty-one percent reported their sexual function improved. That's nothing to joke about." I'll say.

Her advice for other Vagipreneurs is as tough-minded as it is realistic. "There are lots of battles that happen between the big wins—lots of things that go wrong until something goes right. Entrepreneurship, in general, is very hard. You can face high levels of anxiety and ups and downs. We are taking taboo topics and trying to make them mainstream and acceptable. Dealing with a male-dominated society can be especially taxing."

But creating is in Colette's DNA. This is her third start-up, and even when, not *if,* Joylux gets big and successful (she secured $5 million in funding in 2018), she says she will take on another, different role because she loves the process of creating and growing a company. At that point, she will hand it off to somebody else to raise and love.

THE QUESTIONS

Colette Courtion, Joylux, Inc.

- **What is your favorite word?**
  Empower.

- **What is your least favorite word?**
  No.

- **What turns you on creatively, spiritually, or emotionally?**
  Making a difference.

- **What turns you off creatively, spiritually, or emotionally?**
  When people say, "It can't be done." I hate barriers. There is always a way; find a different path. If you're faced with a challenge, there are at least three other ways you can look at it.

- **What sound or noise do you love?**
  My son's laughter.

- **What sound or noise do you hate?**
  Fingernails on a chalkboard.

- **What is your favorite curse word?**
  Fuck.

- **What profession other than your own would you like to attempt?**
  Something in the creative arts—acting or being an artist.

- **What profession would you not like to do?**
  Accountant.

- **If Heaven exists, what would you like to hear God say when you arrive at the Pearly Gates?**
  "You did good."

✳ ALEXANDRA FINE: CEO and Cofounder, Dame Products

"Guys make jokes to my boyfriend. 'Your girlfriend runs a vibrator company. You must not be doing a good job.'"

"When I was six," Alexandra Fine says, "my aunt took me to a drag show. Later, I explained to my class the difference between a drag queen and trans person. I was called home from school and told I couldn't hang out with my aunt anymore."

That was the first of several memorable experiences in Alex's life that made her indignant about how sexual health and wellness issues are handled, but it certainly wasn't the last.

"Then, I took a health class during my junior year of high school. I'd already lost my virginity," she remembers. "I did everything by the book. I found out I had HPV. I had to get a cervical biopsy. I thought I had cancer. And we didn't even *talk* about HPV in health class. I wanted to do a presentation on HPV; I told the teacher I wanted to share my personal experience. And this was a teacher who really cared. What I quickly discovered was that this was a *bad idea*. Don't share your personal sexual experience! The powers that be don't want that information out in high school. But here's the thing; I had *already* helped people. Even at that age, I already knew I had the confidence and a huge mouth to share my personal experiences— and that I could be a strong voice for women.

"My freshman year at Washington University in St. Louis, I told my parents I wanted to be a sex therapist. Although they convinced me not to pursue that, I did take classes in the area— psychology, art and women, gender, and sexuality. After school, I started working in consumer goods. There's a whole industry of consumer goods focused on sexuality. It's a huge opportunity with few people ready to take the challenge on. So, there was no particular, definitive moment that shaped my path," Alex says. "I'm still on it." Dame's first product, Eva, a hands-free wearable clitoral vibrator that is inserted via soft plastic arms that apply gentle tension within the labia during sex, was a runaway success on crowdsourcing platform Indiegogo in 2014. It raised more than $850,000, representing 1,151 percent of its goal—a strong hint that the marketplace was willing to go where the Standards & Practices people fear to tread. (To the best of my knowledge, this was the first sexual health product *ever* funded on Indiegogo.)

Alex's partner at Dame, Janet Lieberman, comes from an engineering background. Together, the two partners approached the development of Eva (and a subsequent product, Fin) as both a creative product development challenge and an exercise in women's empowerment; unsurprisingly, Dame's products are among the few that aren't phallus-shaped.

Even though the business is a success, with Dame's high-quality products occasionally selling out entirely (as I write, the current promotion code on the website is PATIENCE), things occasionally get…awkward. "Oh, gosh, yes. There are moments," Alex says. "For instance, when old white men make 'jokes' like, 'oh, do you do your own product testing?' When someone brings up my personal sex life because of what I do, that crosses a line. It's difficult to explain boundaries; I mean, in any other setting, we are not going to be talking about my masturbation habits."

I'd say. Unless you want to lose your job.

Not that Alex *only* flies solo. She's been dating the same guy since she started Dame with Janet, and that takes a great deal of security.

"He is a great sport. He knows that I like to talk about sex. 'Oh, Alex made a vagina joke!' All of our friends are over it. Now that we have been dating five years, he's incredibly supportive of the business. In the beginning, guys would make jokes at his expense. 'Your girlfriend runs a vibrator company; you must not be doing a good job.'"

Hardly.

I sort of wish that Alex had pulled out the line from *Mean Girls* and said to those guys, "Calling someone stupid doesn't make you any smarter."

Drop the mic, Alex.

THE QUESTIONS

Alexandra Fine, Dame Products

- **What is your favorite word?**
  Plucky.

- **What is your least favorite word?**
  I love things that make people have an emotional reaction, which in turn makes me love the words that make me uncomfortable. Like "discharge" or "pus." I know those are gross words, but I want to pop a pimple now!

- **What turns you on creatively, spiritually, or emotionally?**
  Other people. New people. I get energy from meeting people who are open, kind, comfortable in their own skin. That turns me on in all of those ways, and working with someone like that helps me come up with better ideas.

- **What turns you off creatively, spiritually, or emotionally?**
  When people are narrow-minded. Defensiveness. There is a fine line between cooperation and competition. We are trying to accomplish the same goal. When we remember that, it is amazing. When we forget it, it all falls apart.

- **What sound or noise do you love?**
  Vibrational breathing, deep rumbles; being surrounded by a blanket of sound.

- **What sound or noise do you hate?**
  Metal on metal and the sound of teeth on a fork.

- **What is your favorite curse word?**
  I use "fuck" the most, but "cunt" is the most appropriate word here. For me, I find it sort of empowering that there is a word for my genitalia that has an aggressive connotation. Hard Cs are both comical and commanding.

- **What profession other than your own would you like to attempt?**
  Lifestyle work. I think it would be really cool to have a niche e-commerce store and run it remotely.

- **What profession would you not like to do?**
  I would never want to be a lawyer, the same way anyone I know never would want to be an investment banker. It's not a culture I would like to be a part of.

- **If Heaven exists, what would you like to hear God say when you arrive at the Pearly Gates?**
  "The pool's out back. The lake is down the river. We have all the booze you could ever want. It is going to be a cool time."

✳ WENDY STRGAR: Founder, Good Clean Love

"Sexual health work is the most deeply personal and transformative growth that people can experience. You can't be sexually well if you are not well overall—and vice versa."

Wendy Strgar calls herself a "loveologist." She began her creative journey into the women's health and wellness space in her kitchen when she was looking to reignite the passion in her marriage but had experienced severe reactions to the petrochemical ingredients in commercially available lubricants. So, she turned her attention to formulating her own from organic, natural components, like aloe vera juice, agar from seaweed, the plant-based thickener xanthan gum, and natural flavors. That is what amazes me about so many of these stories and the people behind them; these folks don't sit around waiting for solutions to problems. They create the solutions themselves and build businesses from there.

As a writer, Wendy also took to the web, blogging about what she was learning through the process. Through her work and her writing, she became an advocate for healthier sex, and not just through the products (although the natural ingredients in Good Clean Love's products *do* reduce the irritation that can lead to unwanted and unpleasant side effects, such as itching, burning, and bacterial vaginosis) but also through the process of opening up to and (re)discovering the importance of openness, honesty, and the willingness to be just a little bit self-centered during intimacy.

Wendy's blog, *Making Love Sustainable,* has been going strong for a decade-and-a-half and contains thousands of pages dedicated to women's sexual freedom and pleasure, addressing such high-level topics as communication, mindfulness, pleasure, and positivity. Meanwhile, her book, *Sex That Works*, has achieved success on Amazon, yet she cannot advertise that book on her own Facebook page. And according to Wendy, Facebook has told her it has a "zero-tolerance" policy for the word "sex" in the title of any book. I can't make this stuff up. This has been a reality for years, although I must note here that at least *one* book (I will not name it here, because tattling isn't nice) with "sex" in the title has had an active page on Facebook since July 2010.

"I remember pretty early in the business," Wendy recalls. "I wanted to participate in a United States trade show. Well, as it turned out, if I couldn't advertise on Facebook, I also couldn't represent the United States as a sex company. We are *so* afraid of sex. We don't cover adult topics in adult ways in this country. And yet online, pornography and adult content is estimated to be a full third of content, and it's perpetually increasing. We're terrified of ourselves as sexual beings, and yet all we're left with is pornography, which has almost nothing to do with what we actually do when we are sexual. Sexuality and being sexual are completely different than being sexualized."

As has often happened during the course of writing this book, I am amazed at how often women building totally different kinds of businesses voice the same perspective.

Eventually, Wendy had to move out of her kitchen and into a laboratory when sales started to accelerate. But that's a good problem to have, and she tackled it with the same verve she's tackled every other issue that's arisen with the business—head on, with enthusiasm. The same passion and drive that have kept her writing a blog for fourteen years have also made her a two-time published author. In June 2017, she released her second book, *Sex That Works: An Intimate Guide to Awakening Your Erotic Life*, which drew praise from no less a critical outlet than *The New York Times*.[26]

With characteristic frankness, Wendy says her entry into the business of making her own lubricants was partly serendipitous and entirely based on her own experiences and those of her friends. "I was trying to save my own marriage, initially, and I knew I had to do something. Everything I bought over the counter caused extremely unpleasant reactions. I had small children; simply giving up on our sex life was not an option. So I started making love oils. I got a boost when I gave some to my friends—most of the women I knew were having sex problems too—and there was a huge response to them. Because if you have pain with sex a few times, your brain flips. For women, sex works from the brain down instead of the genitals up."

Wendy eventually realized that scent was another route to arousal. "The brain's limbic system and olfactory systems are entwined and can turn that desire cycle on its head," she says. "An aphrodisiac scent can actually turn arousal into the *leader* of our sexual cycle instead of counting on desire to lead the way."

One of the surprising things that Wendy sometimes hears is, "I don't feel comfortable working for a sex company; I couldn't tell anyone in my family." She is still stunned and saddened by how many people are so distant from their own sexual natures.

Despite such challenges and the fact that it remains a continuous battle to get the word out about the company (see also: every other women's sexual wellness product in North America), Wendy remains undaunted and says Good Clean Love has already been

---

[26] Newman, Judith. "Sex-Ed for Grown-Ups: A Roundup of Relationship Self-Help." *The New York Times*. April 19, 2017. https://www.nytimes.com/2017/04/19/books/review/help-desk-sex-relationship-self-help.html?mcubz=0.

profitable and is on a projected sustainable growth curve into 2020. Before this work, Wendy's previous career was also a calling, not just a job. She was deeply involved in the disability community, doing a great deal of work for the Washington State Department of Developmental Disabilities. "Although few people may see the connection immediately," she says, "I do. Sexual health work is the most deeply personal and transformative growth practice people can experience. You can't be sexually well if you are not well overall—and vice versa. I never started out to make money. I think when you don't use profit as a main input for decision-making, good choices are pretty obvious. Good Clean Love is all about helping people have better sex lives, which is one of the most healing things we can do for ourselves."

Wendy is especially concerned about what's been labeled "hookup culture," which is often divorced from knowing another person and the intimate connection we all crave as a central mechanism of knowing who we are. "It is very concerning," she says. "Hookups aren't a substitute for real intimacy. The kind of sex I believe we crave is the kind when someone looks you in the eye when they are making love to you and shares that kind of depth."

Is she afraid, ever?

"Sometimes. Sometimes I'm am afraid of the ways this latest book I've written will expose my own stories and command me to be even more present to the risks of telling our sexual stories," she says. "But I also know that doing this work is an honor—it is by sharing our past sexual history and traumas that we begin to heal them."

Wow. Brave and creative.

THE QUESTIONS

Wendy Strgar, Good Clean Love

- **What is your favorite word?**
  Love.

- **What is your least favorite word?**
  Politics.

- **What turns you on creatively, spiritually, or emotionally?**
  The pulse of the universe. When you meditate and you learn how to move into the space beyond thought, there is a deep throb that you can tap into—the heartbeat of the universe.

- **What turns you off creatively, spiritually, or emotionally?**
  Business. I hate the way people try to take more. When they don't show up purposefully, both literally and figuratively, people become less than themselves.

- **What sound or noise do you love?**
  Laughter.

- **What sound or noise do you hate?**
  Traffic.

- **What is your favorite curse word?**
  Fuck.

- **What profession other than your own would you like to attempt?**
  I have always wanted to be an energy healer, an inventor, and a painter. Most recently I wish I had studied to be a dolphin trainer.

- **What profession would you not like to do?**
  I have never wanted to have work that is driven by financial numbers, so I would never consider being an accountant or a controller.

- **If Heaven exists, what would you like to hear God say when you arrive at the Pearly Gates?**
  "You have always been loved."

CHAPTER 7

Education: Maximizing Women's Sexual Health and Fulfillment through Knowledge

f I were the empress of the universe with a magical scepter that could rid the world of dangerous clichés, I know exactly which one I'd dispatch first.

"Ignorance is bliss."

No, it's really, honestly *not*. Especially when it comes to women's sexual health and wellness, ignorance may be many things, from fairly benign, to dangerous, to outright deadly. A lack of knowledge today could lead to painful and incurable sexually transmitted diseases, injuries, infections, trauma to the genitourinary or anal tract, increased likelihood of abuse, or even a long, anorgasmic, unfulfilling sex life.

I can think of many words to describe each of those scenarios, but *bliss* is not among them.

From purely a health perspective, the number of American women who don't fully understand their own reproductive systems is staggering. As recently as 2014, a Yale study surveyed 1000 women of reproductive age and the results were both revealing and discouraging.[27] About half of the respondents between the ages of eighteen and forty said they had *never* discussed their reproductive health with a medical provider—*half*! And of those, although nearly 80

---

[27] Peart, Karen N. "The Science of Baby-making Still a Mystery for Many Women." *YaleNews*. January 28, 2014. https://news.yale.edu/2014/01/27/science-baby-making-still-mystery-many-women.

percent reported they had at least some college education, they were remarkably uninformed about issues surrounding female fertility.[28]

- The youngest women, between the ages of eighteen and twenty-four, tended to believe having sex multiple times per day increases the chances of conceiving (it doesn't).

- Women between the ages of thirty-five and forty, as a group, tended to believe that women produce new eggs throughout their lifetime (they don't—a woman is born with all the eggs she will ever produce).

- Sixty percent of women said they believed sex *after* ovulation increases the chances of conceiving, which is actually the opposite of the truth; the two days *before* ovulation are the most favorable days for fertility.

- Forty percent of women reported using the web as their primary source of education about sexual and reproductive health—but the web, being the web, is as full of bad information as it is good information, and quackery abounds.

Then there's this mind-blowing, brain-melting, infuriating fact: only nineteen of twenty-two states that require sex education in public schools require that the information provided in these classes be medically, factually, and technically accurate.[29] "Abstinence-only" sex education is littered with shame and guilt rather than facts, which is why I am not shocked at all by outcomes data that consistently demonstrate such programs result in *less* use of birth control and

---

[28] Rogers, Stephanie. "Reproductive Health Mystery to Many Women." Yale Daily News Reproductive Health Mystery to Many Women Comments. February 4, 2014. https://yaledailynews.com/blog/2014/02/04/reproductive-health-mystery-to-many-women/.

[29] Tassel, Gabrielle Van. "Sex Education or Sex Ignorance?" *The Huffington Post.* May 03, 2015. Accessed September 24, 2017. http://www.huffingtonpost.com/gabrielle-van-tassel/sex-education-or-sex-igno_b_7199708.html.

higher rates of sexually transmitted infections among those students who have gone through them. And I am not making any judgment about when and if people get pregnant, but it is disturbing to learn that upwards of 45% of all American pregnancies are unintended—defined as a pregnancy "that was either mistimed or unwanted."[30] Among all fifty states, only *two* forbid the promotion of religion in sex education classes (if I gave you a full day to guess which they are, you'd probably land on one in a heartbeat and never imagine the other: they're California and Louisiana). Furthermore, this isn't a problem isolated to the United States; a mid-2017 study in the United Kingdom revealed that fully 50 percent of 1,000 men surveyed were unable to correctly locate the vagina (as opposed to the vulva, the clitoris, the uterus, the cervix, or other structures) on an anatomical chart of the female body.[31]

What's the alternative to ignorance?

The power that comes from education, accurate information, and knowledge. The Vagipreneurs I spoke with who are working within the realm of education are working to empower women in all walks of life—from physicians in private practice to individual women in their own bedrooms. They are tirelessly and passionately (no pun intended) laboring to remove the stigma that is so common in the world of women's sexual experiences, health, reproduction, and pleasure. Together with the Vagipreneurs making inroads with technology, creativity, distribution, and their business model, they're working to create a new motto.

Knowledge is bliss.

[30] "Unintended Pregnancy in the United States." Guttmacher Institute. Accessed November 3, 2017. https://www.guttmacher.org/fact-sheet/unintended-pregnancy-united-states.

[31] Allen, Victoria. "Half of Men Cannot Label Where the Vagina Is on a Picture of the Female Body: Poll Finds One in Six Know Nothing about Gynaecological Issues." Daily Mail Online. September 04, 2017. http://www.dailymail.co.uk/health/article-4838456/50-men-label-vagina-picture-female-body.html.

✳ BETTY DODSON, PhD: Pioneering Author and Women's Sex Educator

"What I am saying is that women need some form of direct or indirect clitoral stimulation to have an orgasm. And when we don't, women invariably fake orgasms. Not everyone is going to admit it, but we do it."

At age eighty-seven, Betty Dodson is a bit of a legend in the world of women's sexual education. She calls herself a "fourth-wave feminist," in defiant and intentional contrast to earlier waves of feminism. Already over forty when the 1970s dawned, Betty lived through, saw up close and personal, and too often experienced early waves of feminism as negative toward both sex and men.

An artist by training, in 1968, Betty mounted the first solo show of erotic art; that same year, she also introduced American women to vibrators. Her memoir, *Sex by Design: The Betty Dodson Story,* explores her own extraordinary life, as well as her place alongside some of the biggest names in the history of women's liberation. While others were registering women to vote, or fighting for passage of the doomed Equal Rights Amendment, Betty was teaching women to have orgasms. In groups of up to fifteen at a time. With vibrators.

Another exhibit in Betty's favor as a legend among Vagipreneurs: Very few people on the planet have a masturbation technique named after them. Through her two-hour Bodysex workshops, which began in the sex-positive 1960s, the Betty Dodson Method was born, and it taught women to prolong the pleasurable experience of vibrator-assisted masturbation by placing a towel between the clitoris and the device to dampen the intensity of the vibrations.

"After I was divorced in the 1950s, I had a lover who introduced me to clitoral stimulation during intercourse. I honored that man in my memoir," Betty says. "I was in my mid-thirties, and that experience completely transformed my sex life. All those years I had been struggling to have 'vaginal orgasms.' But when I masturbated, I stimulated my clitoris, and well, naturally, that solved every problem I'd ever had. I started to tell my friends about it. One thing led to another, and then I started to write a book about masturbation, because what I had struggled with—becoming orgasmic and learning what my body responded to—was something almost every other woman I spoke with had also struggled with. Then along came feminism, or as it was called at the time, 'women's liberation,' and I was right in the thick of it, instantly. I self-published that book, *Liberating Masturbation,* in 1974."

Today, nearing her tenth decade of life, Betty says she still loves her vibrator, and she's still active as a sex educator and coach. In 2006, she met her current business partner, Carlin Ross, a former corporate attorney, through a fortuitous interview. The women hit it off and became business partners, creating an online portal, dodsonandross.com, and today the two women facilitate Bodysex workshops together at Betty's Manhattan home.

"Teaming up with Carlin was transformative," Betty says. "She's totally savvy. She got me into social media. She tripled my audience. What a woman. What a dynamo. This combination of feminism and sexuality has created a partnership that's lasted ten years now. It's been brilliant. And it doesn't have much to do with making money at all—not now. I'm in private practice, and Carlin is married and raising a baby. We aren't running the workshops to make money. We're trying to get important information for sexual fulfillment out there, and we want it to be as available as possible to as many people as possible."

One might expect a woman as ahead of her times to have grown up in the same glittering city where she now hosts workshops and posts new content about sexual fulfillment every day, but in fact, Betty's roots are in America's heartland. She grew up in Wichita, Kansas, raised by "the best mother on the planet," as she describes her to this day. But clearly, Betty (and Toto, too) are not in Kansas anymore. Originally, she went to New York City to pursue a career in fashion illustration, spending several years at art school. "I loved that period in my life," she says. "Everybody was so open-minded, liberal, questioning everything. It was exciting. There was no curriculum. When it comes to art, no teacher is droning on at the head of the classroom. You learn by doing. And I got that right away. *You learn by doing.* I think that's obviously a concept I've carried with me through the years. My whole life has been experiential, not theory. I have literally taught millions of women how to have an orgasm through masturbation. You really can't do that through a lecture. Or a video."

Betty also recognizes that sex, for both men and women, is a political minefield—and in the same way she brushed off the sex-negative messages of first- and second-wave feminism, she's having *none* of it. "I don't give a shit if somebody is transgender, or what labels people use. *All* women, straight or LGBT, have a right to orgasm on our own terms, doing what works for us, not trying to live up to Sigmund Freud's concepts or live down to the images and themes of online porn, which promotes the absolute *worst* stuff about sex. What I am saying is that women need some form of direct or indirect clitoral stimulation to have an orgasm. And when we don't, women invariably fake orgasms. Not everyone is going to admit it, but we do it. OK, boys? *Listen the fuck up.*"

Which is not to say Betty didn't have some trying times as a woman nearly half a century ahead of her times. "For the first many years I was involved in this work after I abandoned a successful art career to pursue sex education and liberation, people asked if I was out of my mind. My father was one of them. I would wake up with feelings of dread, fearing I'd ruined my life. But I couldn't stop. I honestly knew, down deep, that this was the key to women's liberation."

For Betty, even today, more than fifty years after she started her work, there are still incredible frustrations. "The worst thing that we do to our girls is to send them out into the world inadequately prepared for sex. We don't teach them about sex. We don't equip them with birth control. And parents, who are either in denial or terrified or religiously or otherwise shut down, think that if they ignore sex, it will go away. Meanwhile, we can't teach this information in the school system. We are withholding vital sexual health information from our girls. And even when we talk about it with them, it's *drenched* in all of this romantic bullshit: 'You'll know when it is the right one; don't masturbate,' all of that. All I can say is, praise the Goddess for the internet. If I had to rely on traditional media, they would shut me down every time. But online, I can tell the truth."

And that's what she does, every day. "Ask Betty" is a featured section on the Dodson and Ross website through which Betty answers between five and ten questions submitted by young people—daily. "I think it's critical for me to stay in touch with the younger generation, because there's a great deal of misinformation out there, and while I won't say I want to censor pornography, women suffer the most from it."

Now that she's officially "made it," peering at the precipice of ninety, what's next for Betty Dodson? "Basking in my marvelous success!" She laughs. "I worked for it, deserved it, got it, and I am fully enjoying it."

That's the spirit, Betty. You can teach us a lot—and not just about masturbation.

THE QUESTIONS

Betty Dodson, Sex and Relationship Coach

- **What is your favorite word?**
  Fuck.

- **What is your least favorite word?**
  Government.

- **What turns you on creatively, spiritually, or emotionally?**
  My clitoris.

- **What turns you off creatively, spiritually, or emotionally?**
  Nothing—everything is stimulating.

- **What sound or noise do you love?**
  My vibrator.

- **What sound or noise do you hate?**
  None of them.

- **What is your favorite curse word?**
  Fuck.

- **What profession other than your own would you like to attempt?**
  I'm not interested in anything else.

- **What profession would you not like to do?**
  Why would I think about what I don't want to do?

- **If Heaven exists, what would you like to hear God say when you arrive at the Pearly Gates?**
  "I have no idea what happens afterward. Dying is agreeing; this one is completely open-ended for me."

✳ RACHEL BREM, MD: Breast Cancer Specialist, Chief Medical Advisor for The Brem Foundation; and ANDREA WOLF: President and CEO, The Brem Foundation

"No disease has higher awareness levels than breast cancer already; ask somebody what a pink ribbon means and almost everybody can tell you, 'It's for the cure.' But women don't know there are screening options that go beyond annual mammograms after the age of forty, and this is life-saving information."

—Rachel Brem

Dr. Rachel Brem's medical credentials are impressive: professor of radiology, vice-chair of radiology, and director of breast imaging and intervention at The George Washington University School of Medicine and Health Sciences. Medical degree from Columbia University. Internship at Sinai Hospital of Baltimore; residency at Johns Hopkins. Additional fellowship training in MRI imaging and breast imaging at Johns Hopkins department of radiology and radiological science.

But it's her personal story that begins to offer glimpses into what drives her work and that of her daughter, Andrea Wolf, CEO of the Brem Foundation—a nonprofit dedicated to the radical belief that women should not die from breast cancer. "I was born in Israel," says Rachel. "My parents had a beautiful love affair. My dad thought he was a head-turner, and my mother, she had a special way about her. She was always singing, always positive. Larger than life. She had bright red hair, enormous green eyes. She filled up a room. Everybody loved her. When I was twelve years old and she was thirty-three, she was diagnosed with breast cancer and disappeared without explanation for a while; I found out much later she'd been told she only had six months to live. Her diagnosis and treatment impacted our lives in a significant way. Although she thankfully lived another forty-four years after that, this beautiful, vivacious woman never fully recovered, and eventually developed ovarian cancer as well. I decided at age twelve that I wanted to do something with my life that would spare other families the trauma that we went through, to minimize the impact of breast cancer on other families, and so I entered college at sixteen, pre-med."

The rest, as they say, is history. But in many ways, it is still being written.

When she was thirty-seven years old and checking out the image quality of a new piece of equipment at work, Rachel inadvertently found something she didn't expect to see; her own breast cancer. She opted for bilateral mastectomy and chemotherapy, placing her in a unique position among many physicians; now she had experienced breast cancer from both sides of the gurney.

Her daughter, Andrea, picks up the thread. "My mother is a living example of the good we can do with early detection. Ninety-five percent of women whose breast cancer is detected in its earliest stages survive and thrive. I am incredibly grateful to my mother for giving me the passion and inspiration to impact the world and empower women to take care of themselves."

Andrea reflects further on some of the coincidences between her formative years and her mother's with matter-of-fact stoicism. "I was twelve when Mom was diagnosed with breast cancer, and my twin sisters were nine, so I was exactly the same age as my mom was when her own mother received her diagnosis. She did a remarkable job of shielding me from the day-to-day reality of treatment; from my perspective, she just had chemo and was gone for a summer. And she has always included me in her work, so talking about breast cancer was normal in our house. We knew my grandmother had also gone through breast cancer, so it wasn't this big, looming, unspeakable thing."

Perhaps because the disease was simply a part of the "family business," so to speak, at age twenty-two, Andrea opted to be genetically tested for the BRCA genetic mutations that make breast and ovarian cancer far more likely to develop. She was ready to know and to change the narrative if need be. When she got her results back, they were positive for the BRCA1 mutation. At age thirty, she made her own decision: prophylactic (preventive) bilateral mastectomy, which evidence has shown to reduce the chances of developing breast cancer by 95 percent in women with this mutation.

Andrea is determined: She will be the first of three generations of her family not to develop breast cancer. When the time comes, she will arm her three daughters with the knowledge to live healthy lives as well, and she wants the same for other women. Andrea went into law and public policy after her preventive procedure, then joined the board of the Brem Foundation, which (despite being named after

Rachel, who serves as its chief medical advisor) was founded not by the Brem family, but by grateful patients. She was chosen to lead the nonprofit only after approaching the board just before it launched a national search for a CEO.

"Our perspective is that no one should die of breast cancer," says Rachel. "Anecdotally, no disease has higher awareness levels than breast cancer already; ask somebody what a pink ribbon means and almost everybody can tell you, 'It's for the cure.' But women don't know there are screening options that go beyond annual mammograms after the age of forty, and this is life-saving information. The disease killed 40,450 women in 2016. Most were diagnosed later in the progression of the disease."

The Brem Foundation is dedicated to a three-pronged approach to tackling the disease.

- **Education**: With programs that serve communities and individuals, the Brem Foundation is working hard to dispel myths and fight back against changing breast cancer screening guidelines, which can cause confusion and breaches of trust between women and the medical community. By encouraging more dialogue about women's real, individual risk factors and personalizing their approach to screening, Rachel and Andrea advocate for an approach that avoids one-size-fits-all generalizations. Personal and family history matters. "We send trained volunteers called 'Brembassadors' into certain communities to get the word out that not all women should rely on one mammogram a year," says Andrea. "And we also offer online webinars and digital education."

- **Physician training:** The foundation offers a fellowship for physician training, producing full-fledged specialist breast radiologists; it is currently the only such program in the nation whose fellows must perform community service as a part of their fellowship training.

- **B-Fund:** While annual mammograms became a covered annual copay-free preventive medical screening with the 2010 passage of the Affordable Care Act, any abnormalities or causes for concern that are identified on screening mammograms (or lumps felt by uninsured women) require further diagnostic imaging and testing. Many women cannot afford such tests. The Brem Foundation's B-Fund pays for such tests to be performed within two weeks, and free screening is available for women in the Washington, DC area who have no insurance.

Andrea says she is especially concerned by the higher incidence of breast cancer and mortality in the Orthodox Jewish community and other conservative religious communities. "It's so taboo, women are literally dying from modesty. There is great stigma associated with being screened for genetic mutations, and that stigma can affect everything from prospects for marriage to decisions about having children, so women don't want to expose themselves. Many simply don't want to know. And we must be open, nonjudgmental, and sensitive to that while also continuing to keep the lines of communication open."

While Rachel and Andrea might have not picked breast cancer as the family business, they have turned lemons into lemonade for their own family and countless others. Rachel's and Andrea's temperaments, their missions, and their spontaneous answers to the questions certainly reinforce that these women are made from the same literal and figurative mold.

THE QUESTIONS

Rachel Brem and Andrea Wolf, The Brem Foundation

- **What is your favorite word?**
  Rachel: Energy.
  Andrea: Joy.

- **What is your least favorite word?**
  Rachel: Grim.
  Andrea: Hate.

- **What turns you on creatively, spiritually, or emotionally?**
  Rachel: My family, unequivocally (children, grandchildren).
  Andrea: Nature.

- **What turns you off creatively, spiritually, or emotionally?**
  Rachel: Unnecessary negativity. It sucks the oxygen out of the room and doesn't help anything. You can't walk around negative all of the time when you are trying to achieve something good.
  Andrea: My mom believes there is always a way to make something work when you are on a mission to do something good. But most people start with "No." That turns me off.

- **What sound or noise do you love?**
  Rachel: The laughter of children and my grandchildren and music.
  Andrea: My kids laughing.

- **What sound or noise do you hate?**
  Rachel: Crying.
  Andrea: Whining.

- **What is your favorite curse word?**
  Like mother, like daughter: Fuck.

- **What profession other than your own would you like to attempt?**
  Rachel: Being a Marine.
  Andrea: Biology entrepreneur; I'd start an awesome wildly successful company.

- **What profession would you not like to do?**
  Rachel: Accountant.
  Andrea: Anything repetitive and boring.

- **If Heaven exists, what would you like to hear God say when you arrive at the Pearly Gates?**
  Rachel: "You done good."
  Andrea: "Within the frailties of humanity, you really tried to be the best that you can be."

✳ Pamela Madsen: Sexual Fulfillment Coach

"Women are not an unsolvable problem; it is as easy as getting rid of shame."

"Talking women out of their panties is a big job," says Pamela Madsen. And it's one that she is still a bit surprised to find herself doing although, in hindsight, it's a completely natural evolution and a combination of her previous career and her personal life.

Read enough stories about woman entrepreneurs and eventually, the name Oprah will appear. This book is clearly no exception. When Pamela made her debut appearance on the nationally televised show, it was in 2010, and she was appearing as an expert on women's fertility. As the founder of the American Fertility Association and its first executive director, she was already a veteran women's advocate, activist, and educator. "I had a whole successful career before I moved on to what I am doing today. I had a black American Express. I flew first-class. I was already nationally known. But ultimately, I was done teaching women how to give birth to children, and once I had done serious work on myself, I knew I wanted to teach women how to give birth to themselves."

As a sex and relationship coach who works exclusively with women, that is precisely what she does today.

Pamela grew up middle-class, the youngest of three children in a liberal Jewish household that was very open and accepting of nearly all things. "We grew up smelling pot and having sex," Pamela remembers. "There was never any shame about sex in our household. Mom took birth control and we knew about it. There were books about sex in the house. It was OK to have sexy feelings, always. But at the same time, there was body shaming, and I was always curvaceous. My mother was a dancer, and I was shamed about my weight." Discomfort with and lifelong negative messages about one's own body, unsurprisingly, are just two of the issues she now works with women to overcome when they engage with her to release all forms of shame and unlock their ability to seek and celebrate their own sexual pleasure.

Pamela says that as a young woman, she remembers thinking her sexuality was so enormous, it needed to be contained within marriage. "Now, of course, I know that women are not an unsolvable problem; it is as easy as getting rid of shame. But back then, I didn't know any better. My husband and I got married at a very young age," she says, "and for many years the only sexual experiences we had were within our marriage." But then something changed. Pamela slowly realized over the course of time that her passions, curiosity, and sexual energy *couldn't* be contained within her marriage.

That's when Pamela conjured up memories of Robin Williams's beloved teacher, John Keating, in *Dead Poets Society*: "*Carpe diem*—seize the day." She turned to gay men's websites and learned about sensual massage. She talks about the entire journey in her memoir, *Shameless*.

"I turned myself into a guinea pig. For ten years, I explored what it was like to feel pleasure through sensual massage therapy, which at the time was all underground and unlicensed. I wanted to stay in my marriage. I didn't do any touching back—this was not romance. Still, what these men helped me do was access parts of my own sexuality and desires that I had held in shame—things that I could not articulate to my partner that would have been too horrifying. This was all before *50 Shades of Grey*. Today it's mainstream and chic to go into a sex store and pick up dominance-submission toys, but it wasn't above ground when I was exploring my own issues, and body shame, and core erotic sexual themes. It took a lot of work to open up and get to the point that I was OK admitting that, like a lot of powerful women, yes, I wanted somebody to tie me up and spank me. It's only kinky the first time. After that, it's just a part of sexual expression."

It took Pamela six months to share the news with her husband. "One night we were making chili, and I told him I'd been seeing sex therapists, and I was into spanking."

He understood. Today, Pamela is still a happily married woman, the mom of two grown sons.

The sensual massage sessions she had gone through helped her find ways to articulate her desires and take away shame; now Pamela is dedicated to helping other women find their own empowerment and do the same. "Women need to uncover and speak their desires' sounds," she says, "but how in God's name do they even start to know what they want? If they've eaten nothing but hamburgers their entire lives, would they even know if they want Thai food? Women are not given the opportunity to explore arousal. Everything is about orgasm. And that's bullshit."

Pamela works with her clients through private sessions conducted through Skype, which makes her practice accessible to clients all over the world, including women in Iran, Bahrain, the United Kingdom, Sweden, Norway, the United Kingdom, Mexico, Panama, and all fifty United States. She also hosts intimate, intensive retreats called Back to the Body, which she describes as a "safe container" staffed with trained, certified professionals in an immersive experience designed to connect a woman with her body, eliminate sexual shame, and discover her erotic desires.

"At a Back to the Body program, we see and hear each other in pleasure. It is women getting to know themselves, even as they get to know each other within a sacred space. I literally get undressed and talk positively about my body. I talk about my relationship with my body. I give an anatomy lesson. Women are provided with kimonos and are invited to come up and share their body stories. We have a flower show; we give women permission to see what vulvas and vaginas look like in all their normal variations. It's all about consent, of course—nobody is touching one another in the group. And during these sessions, it's truly remarkable; when you hear another woman having a breakthrough, others in the group frequently start crying empathetically, because they are deeply moved by her experiencing pleasure. It's a very different dynamic than normal, everyday life because women are so frequently set against each other in competition out there in the 'real world' regarding our appearance and everything else."

There are never more than nine women in a Back to the Body retreat, and they come from every kind of educational, professional, and ethnic background. Pamela says attendees have included physicians, artists, lawyers, single mothers, other sex practitioners, famous women, women who simply are not willing to believe this is all there is, even women who have experienced sexual abuse and are looking for ways to heal from that trauma and re-embrace their sexuality.

The retreats have been a financial success (and interestingly were at break-even from day one). As a business and as Pamela's life mission, this is a source of both pride and relief, because it means her calling is not just sustainable—it is scalable.

"Back to the Body retreats are priced at $6,000, and sometimes it feels hard to sell retreats to women without feeling like a used car salesman when you're in a healing profession, but at a certain point, we did have to make some rules, like a nonrefundable deposit," Pamela says. "I honestly didn't expect this to become a business, but then, I didn't expect to be head of the fertility clinic, either. We never have problems filling retreats, and I want to invest more in Back to the Body. There's demand and women need it. Right now, it's just me. Maybe it'll be a franchise opportunity. Give me a year; I'll let you know."

THE QUESTIONS

Pamela Madsen: Sex and Relationship Coach

- **What is your favorite word?**
  Pleasure.

- **What is your least favorite word?**
  No.

- **What turns you on creatively, spiritually, or emotionally?**
  Adventure.

- **What turns you off creatively, spiritually, or emotionally?**
  Being told I can't.

- **What sound or noise do you love?**
  The sound of women laughing in pleasure.

- **What sound or noise do you hate?**
  A door slamming.

- **What is your favorite curse word?**
  Fuck.

- **What profession other than your own would you like to attempt?**
  Horse trainer or competitive rider.

- **What profession would you not like to do?**
  Cartographer.

- **If Heaven exists, what would you like to hear God say when you arrive at the Pearly Gates?**
  "It is so good to see you."

Chapter 8

Social Impact: Changing the World, One Female at a Time

Every Vagipreneur I have met, whether she or he intends to or not, embarks on a project that will in one way or another create ripples (or even enormous waves) that affect the larger society in which we live. But some go a step farther, aiming from the very beginning to change some aspect of the environment or socioeconomic conditions throughout the world as part and parcel of the mission.

These are the Vagipreneurs who are taking on their work for social impact.

And I know I may occasionally get carried away with my sports and pop culture references, but the more time I spend with these amazing people, here I think of Kurt Russell as coach Herb Brooks in *Miracle:* "Tonight, we are the greatest…team in the world."

I doubt that anybody wakes up one day and declares, in the abstract, "I want to be a socially conscious Vagipreneur." I certainly have not come across any who that started that way. These women's journeys are as unique as they are personal, and they are not limited to those building businesses in the nonprofit sector, although they certainly operate there. Suhani Jalota, who was profiled in the Distribution chapter, certainly also belongs here; so does Cindy Gallop, looking to transform the ways in which the internet presents human sexuality, offering insights into healthy, nonpornographic intimate encounters and a simultaneous opportunity for consensual creators to monetize their shared content. Rachel Brem's educational outreach work fits into this category.

In fact, nearly every Vagipreneur's work has at least some tangential social impact, whether the work offers women new opportunities for personal sexual health and wellness, improved access to reproductive/gynecological health care, or simply novel economic opportunities in the marketplace.

The women I profile in this chapter were deeply motivated by concerns on a global scale. They entered the door through women's health and business, but their view and impact are wider, with potential effects that may one day reach around the planet and impact global human health.

✳ MIKI AGRAWAL: Founder, THINX Period Panties

"When I looked at the market, there had been three innovations during the twentieth century in menstrual health—tampons, pads, and menstrual cups. I thought, there has to be something else we can bring to the table."

What kind of a socio-environmental impact could a lousy little period have on the globe, anyway?

Actually, somebody has done the math already, and it's staggering. According to *Flow: A Cultural History of Menstruation,* the average American woman will menstruate for thirty-eight years and throw away between 250 and 300 lbs. of pads, tampons, and applicators during that time.[32] Using United States Environmental

---

[32] Stein, Elissa, and Susan Kim. *Flow: the Cultural Story of Menstruation.* St. Martin's Griffin, 2009.

Protection Agency (EPA) estimates of lifetime trash production, that's about .05 percent of everything she will ever dispose of into sewers or landfills.

As more consumers opt for green alternatives to nonrecyclable products, it was inevitable that solutions for menstruation would catch up. And while washable cloth diapers have been around forever for infants (we have already seen that washable rags are still in use for women in developing parts of the world as well as in the United States), period panties are relative newcomers to the women's health and wellness space.

Miki Agrawal's Vagipreneurial journey began with a personal catalyst. "I was at a family barbeque with my twin sister defending our three-legged race title," she remembers. "My sister started her period and sprinted to the bathroom. Blood was coming out of her bathing suit bottom, and something just snapped. Because I was also having accidents every month. It was ridiculous. I *hated* pads. They're so fat and bulky. And even with tampons, leaks were staining all of my underwear. And my clothing. *So* frustrating."

That year, Miki had opened a gluten-free restaurant, so it took a while for her to shift her focus to leak-proofing women's periods. She says, "While I spent five years focusing on the restaurant, that incident was always at the back of my mind, and of course, every month, there was always a reminder." A huge soccer fan and former collegiate and semi-pro player (she played for Cornell and the New York Magic), Miki attended the 2010 World Cup as a fan. During that experience, she learned that in the developing world, some girls are still, to this day, missing school a week or more per month because they do not have access to period management products.

"That lit a fire under my ass," she says, with characteristic color and frankness. "My father came to the United States from India with $5; I have a wonderful Japanese mother who came to this country barely speaking English. I live a lucky life partly because of choices that my parents made. They put three children through Ivy League schools and built the American Dream for us. I realized I wanted to do something about this lack-of-access-to-menstrual-products issue. When I looked at the market, there had been three major innovations during the twentieth century in menstrual health—tampons, pads, and menstrual cups. I thought, there had to be something else we could bring to the table."

Beginning in 2011, Miki and her early founding partners at THINX began a three-and-a-half-year journey of research and development, searching for a combination of fabrics that could handle up to two tampons' worth of liquid, but which would also remain comfortable and odor-free. They were in search of a multi-ply design that would be highly absorbent and moisture-wicking with anti-microbial properties. The idea was to find a combination that would allow women to be confident that their panties were a completely reliable backup for tampons or diva cups—not a complete replacement—although several early internet reviewers took the term "period panties" as a straight-up challenge, wearing THINX alone and reporting that they actually *did* perform admirably well under those circumstances, too.

"It felt like it was a game of Sherlock Holmes sometimes," Miki says of those product development days, "asking people to invest their time, finding the right fabrics, having seamstresses make prototypes, and then doing user testing—basically bleeding into them—then washing them, seeing how they held up, then starting over to test new fabrics. Over and over again."

At the same time, they were seeking the right washable fabric technology for THINX, the period panty pioneers were also looking for a way to get into the social giving space in a way that was responsible and sustainable in the long-term. As they looked at other socially conscious companies, they wanted to ensure that THINX's contributions would solve problems, not create unintended consequences or indulge in what Miki wryly calls "white saviorism."

Rather than adopting a social giving model that emulated other companies' endeavors (in which a consumer buys a product and the company gives one away in an impoverished nation—what Miki and many others call the "Toms Shoes model") Miki decided, as an enterprise, to invest in socially engaged businesses located within communities that would benefit from infusions of capital. The first recipient of THINX's give-back investment was AfriPads, a Ugandan enterprise that, following a model much like that of the Myna Mahila Foundation, employs local women (and a few men) to manufacture reusable, washable cloth sanitary pads. This directly empowers girls to remain in school during their periods—thus closing the loop on the issue that had lit that fire under Miki to begin her Vagipreneurial journey in the first place.

THINX Period Panties finally had its "grand launch" in May 2015, and the experience was like catching a rocket in a lasso. "We went viral five times," Miki says. "We went from three employees in 2014 to hiring as fast as we possibly could. I brought in a partner to manage my restaurant business, Wild—yes, the restaurant is still there—you can see the menu and more at eatdrinkwild.com. Basically, I consider myself the chief creative officer across all of these brands, deeply involved in ideation, the brand, and marketing side of things."

What were these "other brands?" Miki turned her attention to nearly everything that goes on behind the bathroom door.

Next, she created Icon panties to help women manage incontinence. "It's time to break this taboo," Miki says. "No adult woman wants to wear diapers. And these are much better products. It's doing extremely well right out of the gate because this is low-hanging fruit. We aren't marketing it to the geriatric market. We don't have to. One in three women experience at least some light bladder leakage, and we think this is the best product on the market to self-manage incontinence."

Her most current product idea is called TUSHY, an enterprise dedicated to bringing designer, affordable, sustainable bidet attachments to toilets in the North American market. Why? Because according to her, traditionally manufactured toilet paper kills enormous numbers of trees unnecessarily (to the tune of fifteen million per year). And its constant use contributes to health problems like hemorrhoids and urinary tract infections. A single roll of toilet paper, Miki points out, requires thirty-seven gallons of water to flush, versus a single pint of water for each TUSHY bidet use. "It's time to get out of the 1800s and into the twenty-first century, isn't it? Water, not dry paper, properly cleans doesn't it? Makes total sense!" She is an evangelist in every sense of the word.

In Asia, full-featured bidet (or "washlet") toilet seats have been in widespread use for decades. While these can be purchased stateside, they are extremely expensive ($350-$900 for full-featured, heated models), making them prohibitive as entry-level introductions to the bidet experience for Americans. By contrast, TUSHY requires no plumbing or electricity, takes ten minutes to install, and retails for $69, making the product an attractive introduction to alternative ways of cleaning up in the bathroom. For people who want to spare trees but who aren't ready to make the leap to a bidet, toilet paper manufactured from renewable bamboo rounds out the TUSHY line of products.

In just a few years, Agrawal went from serving food to serving a woman's comprehensive needs in the bathroom, offering novel and environmentally low-impact solutions for, as she phrases it, "Pizza, periods, pee, and poo."

But Miki's tale is also one that is also ever-unfolding, as are the stories of many Vagipreneurs who push against taboos and boundaries. One of the hard lessons of business is one of the most obvious; not every Vagipreneurial tale has a happy ending. While her creative and leadership work at TUSHY continues, in early 2017, amidst a great deal of publicity, Miki stepped down from her CEO role at THINX after an employee accused her of sexual harassment. (The charge was later dropped after a confidential settlement was reached.) Regarding this experience and her quick bounce back from it, she is philosophical. Interviewed by Megan Bruneau, a psychotherapist writing for *Forbes.com*, she summed up her fearless approach to navigating the stratospheric highs and occasionally subterranean lows that come with the uncertainty of working within the white space of women's sexual health and wellness:

"Often, with a story like mine with this great build-up and takedown...it's like, 'Oh I don't want to expose myself and potentially experience that'...No, this is part of life...I want to skid to death's door sideways and dirty and messed up, and not just do it safely and perfectly and impeccably—with no bruises or bumps along the way. I wanna experience every human emotion; I wanna go through the highs and the lows; and if that's at my expense sometimes, as painful as they are, which they are, then I get to experience it. It's still an experience...And I get to now regale my boy with these stories...like 'and then this happened! And then *this* happened!' And he's waiting to hear the next installment of my story."[33] So are we.

THE QUESTIONS

Miki Agrawal: Founder of Thinx, Icon, and Tushy

- **What is your favorite word?**
  100 percent.

- **What is your least favorite word?**
  Can't.

- **What turns you on creatively, spiritually, or emotionally?**
  Injustice.

- **What turns you off creatively, spiritually, or emotionally?**
  Greed and ego.

- **What sound or noise do you love?**
  The sound of a sigh. Aaaaahhhh.

- **What sound or noise do you hate?**
  Negativity.

- **What is your favorite curse word?**
  Fuck yes!

- **What profession other than your own would you like to attempt?**
  Professional soccer player or Broadway actor.

---

[33] Bruneau, Megan. "5 Steps Former THINX CEO Miki Agrawal Followed To Bounce Back From Adversity." *Forbes.* July 31, 2017. https://www.forbes.com/sites/meganbruneau/2017/07/29/5-steps-thinx-founder-miki-agrawal-followed-to-bounce-back-from-adversity/#61cc1861470d.

- **What profession would you not like to do?**
  Fundraising—asking people for money.

- **If Heaven exists, what would you like to hear God say when you arrive at the Pearly Gates?**
  "Welcome."

✳ MEIKA HOLLENDER: Cofounder and Co-CEO, Sustain

"To me, the way my parents did business was just the way things are, the way things should be—doing business the right way, improving people's health and lives, taking care of the planet, caring for the environment. It's all wrapped up together."

The word is right there, front and center. It's the philosophy. It's the brand name. *Sustain.*

Meika Hollender, who cofounded Sustain Natural—a company dedicated to producing sexual health products that are fair-trade, vegan, cruelty-free, carcinogen-free, fragrance-free, and harmful-chemical-free—got a very early start in the world of socially responsible products. In fact, as an infant, she modeled organic cotton diapers. The competition for that gig wasn't terribly stiff, considering her parents, Sheila and Jeffrey Hollender, are the cofounders of Seventh Generation, an iconic brand in the sustainability space. And it was working with them to launch organic cotton tampons that got Meika's feet wet in the women's sexual and reproductive health category.[34]

---

[34] Drewis, Deena. "Portrait of a Girlboss: How Meika Hollender Is Making Sex Healthier for Everyone." Girlboss Media: Redefining Success for Ourselves. November 1, 2016. https://www.girlboss.com/girlboss/2016/11/1/portrait-of-a-girlboss-how-meika-hollender-is-making-sex-healthier-for-everyone.

"I have always been passionate about women's reproductive health issues," Meika says, "When I graduated with my MBA from NYU's Stern School of Business in 2014, my dad came to me with an idea: sustainable condoms. But I actually had a bigger idea. Why not start a company with him, dedicated to bringing sustainable products to market dedicated to the entire spectrum of sexual health? I knew we could build something meaningful. I've always believed companies should create good in the world, so it was natural for me to pursue that." Meika points out that conventional versions of the products Sustain manufactures and sells, such as tampons, condoms, lubricants, and hygienic vaginal wipes, contain materials and ingredients that are known to be toxic and carcinogenic. "I knew there was a huge opportunity to bring healthier products to women—better, safer, nontoxic, nonharmful sexual health and wellness products. What I didn't realize, at least at the outset, was how controversial working within this space can be and how many uphill battles we would face."

When Sustain earned its first piece of video press, and Meika was featured online, she experienced the kind of internet comment trolling that knocks some people to their knees. What was the catalyst? A freckle on her lip.

"Yep. Can you believe it? After being incredibly excited about getting our first piece of press born into the world, the first comments were that I should be *using* condoms, not *selling* condoms. The implication, of course, was that I had herpes on my lip. And until then I hadn't thought about what it meant to be the face of a sexual wellness company. That was one of the first times I experienced attempted shaming, and it had precisely the opposite effect the commenters wanted. It didn't work. Now I'm doubly determined to stop slut-shaming. That experience simply made me more motivated, more passionate about what we do at Sustain every day."

A great deal of the work Meika does through Sustain today, in fact, is targeted at destigmatizing sexual health and opening up conversations about it. The Sustain website's tagline as this book is being written is "Think with Your Vagina"—bold, in your face, and unapologetic. Just like the company's shamelessly feminist cofounder. In 2018, she published a book on the subject written in the same way, with the same purpose. *Get on Top: Of Your Pleasure, Sexuality & Wellness (A Vagina Revolution)* is targeted at young women who are swimming in a sea of information, intimidation, and fear, with the goal of arming them with all the facts they need to help them make smart, safe, empowered sexual choices.

Sustain is also dedicated to a generous give-back commitment, donating 10 percent of its pretax earnings to organizations that provide access to women who otherwise would not be able to afford reproductive health services. "My mom has always been involved with Planned Parenthood," Meika says, "and I think as a result, I never fully understood how controversial it was. To me, the way my parents did business was just the way things are, the way things should be—doing business the right way, improving people's health and lives, taking care of the planet, caring for the environment. It's all wrapped up together."

Meika also enjoys a different kind of personal sustainability: her sense of humor. "I think the funniest thing about this entire experience so far was when we got a complaint that our condoms were too small. Believe it or not, that's a pretty common complaint, and most condom manufacturers get it at one time or another; it's psychological, and usually the men who make that complaint aren't putting them on correctly. Anyway. My mom is hilarious. She sent an email with a photo of one of our condoms with six lemons inside of it to the entire team as a Reply All, asking 'How could this be too small?' It's a true family business, and moments like that are golden."

Meika is proudest of one of the changes she's been able to make that has a completely noncommercial, socially conscious component: A pledge for women to practice safe sex, hosted at letsgetontop.com. "Almost half of all American pregnancies are unplanned, and only 62 percent of women of reproductive age are even using contraception," she says. "For every woman who signs the pledge, we send her three condoms and donate another to a woman in need. I didn't ever think of being an entrepreneur and not having an altruistic component. I'm extremely proud of this pledge. Even if my business were shut down tomorrow, I have made a contribution." Because the world of women's health and wellness is so small and tight-knit, it should come as no surprise that the humorous and sassy promotional video for the "Let's Get On Top" pledge features other Vagipreneurs as well.

THE QUESTIONS

Meika Hollender, Cofounder, Sustain Natural

- **What is your favorite word?**
  Feminine.

- **What is your least favorite word?**
  No.

- **What turns you on creatively, spiritually, or emotionally?**
  Live music and acupuncture (not at the same time).

- **What turns you off creatively, spiritually, or emotionally?**
  Stress and negativity.

- **What sound or noise do you love?**
  My boyfriend opening the door when he comes home from work.

- **What sound or noise do you hate?**
  Somebody chewing on ice.

- **What is your favorite curse word?**
  Fuck.

- **What profession other than your own would you like to attempt?**
  Working for Planned Parenthood or being a pure activist.

- **What profession would you not like to do?**
  Coding.

- **If Heaven exists, what would you like to hear God say when you arrive at the Pearly Gates?**
  "Thank you."

✳ BETHANY EDWARDS: Cofounder and CEO, Lia Diagnostics, Inc.

"Sometimes it gets incredibly frustrating, being treated like a little girl with a new pregnancy test she is trying to sell."

"There is a social narrative," says Bethany Edwards, "that little girls want to be mothers from the day they are born. That is absolutely, definitely not always the case. Some women do. Some women don't. And until now, pregnancy tests have been—well, let's say they're problematic if you are trying to be completely private about them in your home. This is a subject that people simply do not want to talk about—unplanned pregnancy, and especially *unwanted* pregnancy. But we should be talking about it."

Bethany is armed with facts, and they're familiar. Nearly half of American pregnancies are unplanned, which encompasses both unwanted or mistimed pregnancies.[35] Of those, about fifty percent end in abortion. Or how about another statistic that's even less frequently discussed—according to a study published in the June 2011 issue of *Journal of Obstetrics and Gynecology*, roughly 60 percent of women seeking abortions in the United States between 2001-2008 were already mothers.[36] "So, this pregnancy test, which is about the size of a credit card, is 100 percent biodegradable and flushable," Bethany says. "It's for the thirteen-year-old who lives in her parents' house and does not want somebody to find it wrapped up in toilet paper in the garbage, or who is afraid of smuggling it out of the bathroom to another trash can, or out of the house entirely. It's for the woman who is struggling to get pregnant and doesn't want a reminder in the trash every day. It's for women who want the freedom to share news about pregnancy their way, in their own time. It's for transgender people, who still face considerable issues when they choose to become pregnant after transitioning. I didn't originally conceive it as a product to be used by people who are looking strictly for privacy, though. Did you know that three million pounds of unrecycled plastic and digital components from pregnancy tests end up in landfills every year?"

---

[35] "Unintended Pregnancy in the United States." Guttmacher Institute. September 20, 2017. https://www.guttmacher.org/fact-sheet/unintended-pregnancy-united-states.

[36] Jezer-Morton, Kathryn. "Two Kids, An IUD, and Then, An Abortion." *Jezebel*. February 18, 2016. http://jezebel.com/two-kids-an-iud-and-then-an-abortion-1758815386.

Like nearly every Vagipreneur I interviewed during the writing of this book, Bethany did not intentionally set out on her quest to become a Vagipreneur—in her case, "The Pregnancy Test Lady." In fact, she is still getting used to that title—one that occasionally chafes, truth be told.

"Oh, absolutely, there's an aspect of not being taken seriously about the innovation regarding this product, or being constantly questioned about it from a business perspective," Bethany says. "Sometimes it's incredibly frustrating, being treated like a little girl with a new pregnancy test she is trying to sell."

Going up against giants in the $366 million United States home pregnancy test industry, it's not surprising that some people don't understand or believe Bethany and her three cofounders are ready to reshape the landscape. That's exactly what this disruptive new technology may be able to do in a space that has not changed significantly for decades. And Bethany has earned the interest and early faith of some heavyweight backers, including Cindy Whitehead, who as the iconic cofounder and CEO of Sprout Pharmaceuticals shepherded the "female Viagra" libido drug Addyi through its FDA approval process. In 2016, Whitehead started a funding incubator, The Pink Ceiling, for women-helmed companies creating products for other women; Lia Diagnostics earned backing through that channel and more. Bethany has also received some financial backing from DreamIt Ventures, a digital health accelerator, and Ben Franklin Technology Partners, an early supporter. "We have raised a total of $2.5 million so far," Bethany says, "and we will need more to bring the product to a broad market to ramp up manufacturing and marketing."

There are also implications for a biodegradable pregnancy test in underdeveloped parts of the world, and a woman's right to access private information about the status of her own reproductive health is paramount in Bethany's sense of mission.

"I grew up in a religious, Christian environment; my mother wasn't a big fan of birth control and we frequently went to church," she says. "I think that had a definite effect on the direction of my philosophy and my thinking. We have *got* to ease up on the judgment. We have to give women the freedom to make choices for their own lives. There is so much infighting. We need to develop our ability to empathize. People tend to want to boil everything down to black-and-white, but decisions about fertility are so much more complex than that."

While Lia Diagnostics' flushable, cellulose-based test was not yet available for purchase when I interviewed Bethany, in December 2017, the product has received clearance from the United States FDA, paving the way for market entry. Its transformative potential for women's autonomy and privacy, both in America and globally, as well as its patented ability to reduce the waste associated with pregnancy tests and other single-use diagnostic kits, points to yet one more way Vagipreneurship is good for women—and good for the planet.

THE QUESTIONS

Bethany Edwards: Cofounder and CEO, Lia Diagnostics, Inc.

- **What is your favorite word?**
  Creativity.

- **What is your least favorite word?**
  Hate. Oh and many others—history, promiscuous, hemorrhoid, polenta, and pus.

- **What turns you on creatively, spiritually, or emotionally?**
  Problem-solving and self-expression.

- **What turns you off creatively, spiritually, or emotionally?**
  When too much structure becomes inhibiting—when things are so ingrained that they can't be changed. Rules without reason.

- **What sound or noise do you love?**
  A babbling stream.

- **What sound or noise do you hate?**
  Car horns, ambulances, and police vehicle sounds.

- **What is your favorite curse word?**
  I say "fuck" too often.

- **What profession other than your own would you like to attempt?**
  Biomimicry—solutions that are nature-based, 360-degree-based solutions.

- **What profession would you not like to do?**
  Factory worker.

- **If Heaven exists, what would you like to hear God say when you arrive at the Pearly Gates?**
  "Welcome."

SECTION 3

Coming Attractions

Chapter 9

Future Business Trends in Women's Sexual Health and Wellness

My journey as I interviewed dozens of women (and some men) to come up with a cross-section who could represent Vagipreneurs young and old, in industries from intimate fashion to sex toys to finance, is one that has been transformative for me, personally. What started as a hope to interview ten people has exploded into more than three dozen interviews (less than half of which appear here—so fingers crossed, more to come).

To return to an early theme, I am and always have been a pop culture nut. I am one of those people who knows every star—OK, maybe not every seventeen-year-old YouTube sensation—but I'm familiar with and a huge fan of all the biggies, whether they're primarily seen in movies, on television, or on Broadway. Suffice it to say that if a person's photo is in *People* magazine, I'll be able to tell you who it is, what he or she is famous for, and probably who he or she is married to, dating, or just broke up with.

That means every year, I look forward to the annual lifecycle event that is red-carpet viewing, Oscar watching, and real-time analysis with my mom, sister, and friends. But even more importantly, red carpet and award season has recently become a marker for me as a Vagipreneur; it marks a measuring point when I can see how much progress we are making in the discussion of female sexual health and wellness.

So, what is the connection?

Just a few years ago, our company was excited about what we thought would be a huge publicity break. Zestra was going make its big debut in celebrity nominee gift bags (you know, those almost absurdly valuable bundles of swag for people who already have tons of stuff) at a major awards show. It wasn't the Oscars, but it was *really big*, just the same. Back at Zestra headquarters, we felt as if we had finally arrived. Visions of champagne and caviar danced in our heads. *National coverage! Our products in the hands of celebrities! Dazzled paparazzi! The whole nine yards!*

Then, in the final moments before the nominee swag bags were finalized and stuffed, the powers that be decided that our product was inappropriate. It "might make people uncomfortable," they said. And just like that, we were out.

Now mind you, these nominees are people who routinely perform nude sex scenes in which men wear nothing but a piece of cloth that's called a "modesty sock," and nobody was going to ask them to whip out the product right there on the red carpet for a live product evaluation. But never mind logical arguments.

The ruling was final. No dice (well, there may have been dice, but no Zestra in the gift bag). Our red carpet dreams were crushed.

What hypocrites.

Then in 2016, the pre-award-show airwaves and social media caught on fire, and the reason was…celebrity swag bags.

Controversy had erupted over some of the items in the gift bags that Distinctive Assets had created and delivered for the Oscars. The company describes its bags as "a blend of fabulous, fun, quirky, and indulgent items meant to thrill and pamper those who may have everything money can buy, but still savor the simple joy of a gift." And what was the thrilling, pampering item that set keyboards aflame and tongues wagging in 2016?

It was Nuelle's female arousal device—Fiera—and wow, did it *ever* get some people aroused.

The Academy of Motion Picture Arts and Sciences (AMPAS)—the organization that gives out those golden statuettes—went nuts (code for "seeking legal remedy"), saying Fiera and some other products in the gift bag were *giving Oscars a bad name*. The spat was eventually settled out of court, with Distinctive Assets arguing their gift bags are no more and no less "officially sanctioned" by AMPAS than the gowns and jewels celebrities wear on the red carpet.

Seriously, Hollywood, get over yourself.

The next year, Distinctive Assets created yet another fabulous bag of tricks, valued at more than $200,000, containing the standard luxurious offerings: for example, access to a luxury ranch with eighteen bedrooms and great food. Or, if ranch living wasn't a recipient's style, he or she could enjoy Classic Women's Week at The Golden Door spa and resort in Southern California or time at a villa in Kauai. But in the tradition of defying convention, Distinctive Assets also selected a product called Elvie for inclusion in the bag.

What was the big deal *this time*?

Elvie is described as a small yet powerful exercise tracker for the pelvic floor, promising something more lasting than the Oscar news cycle—better core strength, control, and yes, even better sex.

Lo and behold, *this time the Academy didn't go nuts*.

As an optimist, I am choosing to believe this is just one more sign that indicates American society's increasing comfort level (albeit from a very low baseline) with conversations about female sexual health. Thanks to the fearlessness and tenacity of the people

I've profiled in this book as well as many others toiling away in the often frustrating and thankless field of women's sexual health and wellness, one of the inevitable consequences I'm looking forward to, both personally and professionally, is the snowball effect.

There are already enough Vagipreneurs out there working to create new business models, creative solutions, technologies, distribution channels, and social change to start that ball rolling downhill faster and faster. And as it does, it will inevitably grow larger and larger.

Right now, we are still at the very top of the hill, and the ball has just started to roll. But as it picks up momentum, stand back. These folks cannot be stopped.

I want to be part of the team cheering along when the snowball becomes enormous and unstoppable. And the doubters will have to jump out of the way to survive.

CHAPTER 10

Spotting Trends

Evaluating Opportunities in the White Space

With very few exceptions, entrepreneurial ventures, including those in the Vagipreneurial space, include several similar and fundamental milestones and critical steps:[37]

1. **Identifying an unmet market need, challenge, desire, gap, social problem, or opportunity** for a transformational change in the way people interact or behave

2. **Developing, creating, or acquiring a realistic and compelling solution** that addresses the unmet need or opportunity

3. **Evaluating the competitive landscape**, which includes the potential customer's options from literally "do absolutely nothing" to "purchase a competitor's product for reasons X, Y, and/or Z," with special attention to those aspects of the solution that establish a compelling and sustainable competitive advantage

4. **Creating a financial plan for commercialization** of the venture, taking into account the costs to develop, sustain, and grow the business (whether it is engaged in product or service delivery); this includes demonstrating a pricing and revenue

---

[37] "Learning: Evaluating an Opportunity." *The Duke Entrepreneurship Manual: A Resource for Entrepreneurs.* Accessed September 24, 2017. https://sites.fuqua.duke.edu/dukeven/new-venture-guidelines/evaluating-an-opportunity/.

structure and growth potential that will convince financial backers that the business has long-term potential for success

5. **Assembling a team** with the skills, talents, passion, and drive to execute on the plan, along with the flexibility to respond quickly to rapidly changing conditions—a virtual given in any start-up

And certainly, there are many more. All of the Vagipreneurs I interviewed for this book went through these steps (and more) in one form or another, and, as with every entrepreneur's story, some have already reached a happy ending—a successful product rollout, a growth spurt, an acquisition, a sustaining partnership, or even just a comfortable (if hectic) sales pace.

But statistically, others may yet find themselves among the long list of start-up casualties. Conventional wisdom and the best estimates available in the popular press tell us that nine out of ten new business ventures fail. The reasons, according to an analysis of more than 100 start-up postmortems written by founders themselves and published by *Fortune* magazine, are worth considering and taking to heart for those who have ideas to bring into the women's sexual health and wellness space.[38]

- Forty-two percent of new businesses failed because the **product or service they were trying to sell failed to find or meet a market need**—the company led with the *product,* not the *customer,* in mind.

- Twenty-nine percent simply **ran out of cash** before they could reach critical sales mass and hit a break-even point.

---

[38] Griffith, Erin. "Startups Are Failing Because They Make Products No One Wants." *Fortune.com.* March 02, 2015. http://fortune.com/2014/09/25/why-startups-fail-according-to-their-founders/.

- Twenty-three percent reported their companies failed because they **hadn't been able to assemble the right team** to operationalize the venture.

- Nineteen percent **lost out to the competition**.

- Eighteen percent **weren't able to overcome pricing or cost issues**.

- Seventeen percent admitted to releasing a **subpar product**.

- Fourteen percent assigned responsibility for their start-up's failure **to bad marketing**—the same proportion that admitted they had **ignored customers**.

- Thirteen percent said their product or service introduction was **poorly timed**.

- The remainder of founders attributed failures to pivots gone bad, poor locations, a lack of passion, legal problems or challenges, failure or lack of investor interest, burnout, and/or a failure to fully leverage advisors or a network of peers.

From my own experience, I also know if I asked 100 more entrepreneurs, I might hear 100 additional reasons.

What's the takeaway?

Entrepreneurship and Vagipreneurship can be challenging enterprises. In this white space, created by thousands of years of social stigma and taboos, women—the customer base for all such enterprises—generally aren't aware of their options. The ability to get word out in the commercial landscape is shaped by outdated gag rules within mainstream advertising, as well as marketing channels that simultaneously and paradoxically welcome full-throated promotion of products that enhance the experience of men's sexuality. These artificial limits can be frustrating and infuriating, but like all stressors, they bring out the fight-or-flight response, and successful Vagipreneurs *fight*.

If I noticed one common quality among the people I interviewed for this project, in fact, it was their fighting spirit. There aren't many shrinking violets among them. (Did you notice a common favorite curse word? Very few held back; it's not a "Miss Manners" sort of crowd.) Knock a Vagipreneur down, and she'll be back on her feet within a microsecond, more motivated, more passionate, *ready, able, and willing to take on the next challenge*—again and again and again. You remember—no time outs, no substitutions!

I have no doubt that the American women's suffragists, who began their quest for the female right to vote with a resolution at the first women's rights convention in 1848 at Seneca Falls, New York, knew they were in for a long, hard slog. But I don't think they had any idea it would take almost *fifty years* to get there.

As I reflect on Betty Dodson's fifty years of work to help women claim their right to sexual pleasure, and then look at the Vagipreneurs walking in her footsteps, from Alex Fine to Colette Courtion to Cindy Gallop to Pamela Madsen, I see generations of women standing on each other's shoulders, declaring bravely and defiantly in words and deeds that we need—we *deserve*—solutions.

When I look at the businesses being started and growing, such as the potentially revolutionary and liberating disposable pregnancy tests developed by Bethany Edwards, or the dual employment/distribution model of Suhani Jalota's Myna Mahila Foundation, I see women's sexual health and wellness work as an act of entrepreneurial empowerment.

These pioneers are the economic equivalent of suffragists marching for the vote more than 100 years ago, risking violent disapproval and social sanction from conservative quarters.

And when I see Tracy Warren forming a venture capital firm solely dedicated to funding women's and children's health and wellness ventures, I think, "Aaaaah. At last. We are arriving. It's our time."

While Vagipreneurs are certainly capitalistic, driven by numbers, and attentive to spreadsheets or P&Ls, they also find inspiration closer to home. They talk to their friends and family, or they look around their hometowns or regions, and they find a glaring, gaping, unaddressed need. Then they get to work—asking questions, raising money, building solutions, and putting them out into the world.

In addition to personal networks, experiences, hometowns, and family circles, where else can women (and men—I am still interviewing for this ongoing project, and I have interviewed men as well) look to find opportunities to build businesses?

Ideas for businesses are everywhere. Women are quite open about expressing their dissatisfaction with the status quo and venting their frustrations when it comes to sexual health and wellness if you know where to look. Free sources of early inspiration for business opportunities in the white space aren't hiding behind brick walls. It turns out women can be open about expressing their dissatisfaction and need for better solutions on some social media platforms.

Exhibit 1: Dating and hookup apps, Facebook, and even Twitter have become notoriously hostile places for women who aren't absolutely *delighted* to receive unsolicited photos of men's…junk. On nearly every dating platform, an astonishing number of women report being verbally abused and sometimes threatened when they decline the "opportunity" to meet men in whom they are not interested. And generally, when they report the abuse, women say they receive no help from the platform other than "suck it up/it's the internet/ignore them/block them." So, they complain—loudly, repeatedly, daily—to each other. In the aftermath of #metoo and other powerful emerging women's advocacy movements, I predict this will remain a market opportunity screaming for a solution (some are attacking this problem as we speak). Somewhere out there will be a multimillion (or billion) dollar market opportunity in search of feasible commercial solutions—a safe platform that does not tolerate harassment and abuse. When it comes to dating and hook-up apps (here's looking at you, Tinder) it's not that women don't welcome casual sexual encounters—it's that random, unasked-for dick pics aren't the mood-setters and conversation starters women are looking for, and when a woman says "No," she isn't asking to be called names or to be threatened or insulted. Whoever solves this problem first is not only going to make a lot of money—she (or he) is also going to make a lot of people, male and female, LGBTQ or otherwise, *very* happy.

Exhibit 2: Did you know about the hashtag #periodproblems on Twitter? Well, it exists. And if you're an aspiring Vagipreneur and you're fishing for product ideas, then you might run across useful tweets that spur creative concepts you may *never* have come up with on your own. Simple things like, "I refuse to wear nice pajamas to bed when I haven't had my period in a while." Solutions? I don't know—*you tell me*. THINX has a head start, but that's just one idea in a potential sea of them. Maybe in a year or so I'll interview you, then blog about you and your new business. Other women use the hashtag (consistently) to bemoan monthly cramps and emotional trials and tribulations of PMS, which is heartbreaking when there are now forms of hormonal birth control like Seasonale, Jolessa, and Quasense, all of which can reduce periods to quarterly events.

For Vagipreneurs, sources of inspiration and product/service ideas tend to come from places closer to home than for other people who start businesses. Vagipreneurs don't have their heads in the clouds. We don't dream in code, hard assets, buildings, or assembly lines. Our line of sight, our focus, and our inspirations are women. They are our mothers, daughters, sisters, aunts, cousins, and friends, and we often begin our journeys right at home, in our living rooms, over glasses of wine at happy hour, on our computers, or at the gym.

Often, when I speak to groups about this exciting space, they ask me to identify the forthcoming trends that I see emerging in the next few years. While many have been mentioned already, some bear repeating and summarizing.

- **Vagipreneurial business leaders speak the language of their customers.** They have deep insights and understandings about problems in women's lives. And importantly, the solutions they source and champion are directly born from and respond to those problems.

- New Vagipreneurial businesses reflect a keen awareness that, while women's lives are complex, and their bodies are complex, **solutions to these problems might actually be simple**—new materials, new distribution channels, or better education.

- Vagipreneurs have taken the focus away from dealing with a particular situation, e.g., menstruation, and have shifted to **looking for physiological or emotional commonalities across the stages of a woman's life.**

- **These businesses are solving *old* problems**—issues that women have dealt with for a long time (maybe even for centuries). What is *new* are the solutions.

- **Solutions come in many different forms, shapes, and sizes**—new approaches, devices, apps, connectivity between systems, monitoring—the list goes on.

- But far and away, the most fascinating part of this study to me was learning that today, different kinds of founders are building **different kinds of companies**. They are focused on doing well and doing good—making money and giving back—participating in conversations while changing our vocabulary.

With the same womanly grit that gets us through #periodproblems, we can (and do, and will) bring new solutions to the market. Of these ventures, some will succeed. Many more will fail. Not every story has a happy ending. We don't all end up going to Disneyland after the proverbial Super Bowl victory. But we all have adventures along the way, and every one of our stories is worth telling, and hearing, and repeating. All of our lessons learned along the way are worth sharing, so the next generation of women and men who choose to take on work in the women's sexual health and wellness white space will do so with more knowledge, more support, more case studies, and more best practices.

Here's to shattering taboos through Orgasmic Leadership. I wish you all the success in the world.

ABOUT THE AUTHOR

Rachel Braun Scherl is the managing partner and cofounder of SPARK Solutions for Growth, a strategic consultancy that focuses on growing businesses and brands. Throughout her career, Rachel has worked with leading companies including Johnson & Johnson, Pfizer, Merck, Bayer, and Allergan, to drive revenue growth across a range of categories, with a focus on female health.

As a Vagipreneur, Rachel works with entrepreneurs and business leaders focusing on women's sexual health, reproductive health and wellness, which has the potential to explode into a multi-billion dollar market.

As a professional speaker, Rachel annually enlightens thousands of corporate leaders, entrepreneurs, students, and investors on how to profit from the coming surge in women's sexual health and wellness in addition to speaking about leadership, entrepreneurship, and women in business.

On a personal note, Rachel adores family, movies, pop culture, comedy, cross-training, travel, and watching college squash. She lives with her husband of twenty-eight years in the New York City area. Her two adult children (who prefer to remain nameless when they are mentioned near anything "Vagipreneurial") are making their way in the world of business and college.

Orgasmic Leadership is Rachel's first book.

Acknowledgments

I have always fantasized about giving an acceptance speech at an awards show, when the winner sounds humble, eloquent, appreciative and for that one moment in time, totally at peace with the world—of course, not one of the unfortunate speeches in which somebody forgets everyone's names and doesn't mention the kids.

So, for a moment (after countless hours watching and evaluating others), here is my speech. And I am acknowledging in advance that if I were actually on a stage at an awards show, the music would cut in and try to get me off the stage before I was done. But this is my moment.

By completing and publishing this book, I have achieved a lifelong dream (which will be made better if I meet Oprah or get on *The Today Show*). People have always told me that I am a good storyteller, which is certainly made easier by the amazing experiences, people, and conversations I have had in my life.

First, to the real-life characters in this book, some of whom have been clients, many friends and a few I have only had the privilege of getting to know for the purpose of interviewing for this book: I am awed to be in a group that includes all of you. Your passion, creativity, immense talent, range of skills, discipline, and focus inspire me. You make me want to keep fighting City Hall.

To my husband, we have always told the kids that the most important choice they will make is who to spend their lives with. I certainly chose well, and you always took care of the "stuff." You are masterful as a partner, friend, cheerleader, roommate, collaborator, and parent. You are the soul of our family.

To my children, who are now adults, thank you for not running away from home when I started talking about vaginas so many years ago.

To my first child, my only daughter: You came into this world as an independent, strong, thoughtful, caring, driven, courageous person and have taken all those amazing gifts into your adult life. You honor us by focusing every day on being a good, caring person, the kind to whom others look for guidance, and in having a good name. You have brought pride to ours.

To my baby and only son: You are steady, clear-thinking, and funny. You have been comfortable in your own skin from the day you were born. You are constantly learning, thinking, reading, and you question science and the universe. But you never question who you are or where you come from. You make us smile.

Dad, you are with me literally every day. I hear your voice, your laugh, your favorite stories. Mom, you are a person of amazing, strength, compassion, and ridiculous patience. You have both been part of every great moment of achievement, picked me off the floor in moments of despair, and literally have been the wind beneath my wings.

Mary, my longtime business partner and forever friend, you helped me grow as a person, a professional and a mother. You are my reliable sage. Look what we were able to build together.

To my in-laws, Mom and our recently dearly-departed Pops, you welcomed me into your family as if I had been there all along. It is a source of pride for me to share your name and your son.

Auntie Dots, my sister, confidante, and medical advisor (unlicensed), our relationship and laughter have been a guidepost in my life. To my siblings-in-law, you are loving, opinionated, and full of life. This family is a team I am proud to be a member of.

To my nieces and nephews, thank you for the unanimous vote selecting me as your favorite aunt. While the votes might not all be in, I figure this is my pretend speech, and who is going to argue with me?

To my friends, old and newer, near and far, even when you don't have any idea where I am traveling to or what I am doing, you always energize me.

To Karen Kahn, thank you for uttering the words, Orgasmic Leadership, in a meeting and setting this whole thing in motion.

And finally, from the bottom of my heart, a huge thank you and fist-pump to my editor, Denise Montgomery, who turned me from a person who wanted to write a book into an author, and my publisher, Henry DeVries, who told me that I had a story to tell. It was a stroke of good luck the day you both walked into my life.

References

"The 2013 State of Women-Owned Businesses Report Commissioned by American Express OPEN." http://www.womenable.com/content/userfiles/2016_State_of_Women-Owned_Businesses_Executive_Report.pdf.

Alba, Davey. "Finally, You'll Be Able to Track Your Period in iOS." *Wired*. September 09, 2015. https://www.wired.com/2015/09/finally-youll-able-track-period-ios/.

Allen, Victoria. "Half of Men Cannot Label Where the Vagina Is on a Picture of the Female Body: Poll Finds One in Six Know Nothing about Gynaecological Issues." Daily Mail Online. September 04, 2017. http://www.dailymail.co.uk/health/article-4838456/50-men-label-vagina-picture-female-body.html.

AP. "Texas Ban On Sex Toy Sales Overturned." *CBSnews.com*. February 14, 2008. https://www.cbsnews.com/news/texas-ban-on-sex-toy-sales-overturned/.

Bruneau, Megan. "5 Steps Former THINX CEO Miki Agrawal Followed To Bounce Back From Adversity." *Forbes*. July 31, 2017. https://www.forbes.com/sites/meganbruneau/2017/07/29/5-steps-thinx-founder-miki-agrawal-followed-to-bounce-back-from-adversity/#61cc1861470d.

Burns, Janet. "How The 'Niche' Sex Toy Market Grew Into An Unstoppable $15B Industry." *Forbes.* August 12, 2016. https://www.forbes.com/sites/janetwburns/2016/07/15/adult-expo-founders-talk-15b-sex-toy-industry-after-20-years-in-the-fray/#662d78215bb9.

Chalabi, Mona. "The Gender Orgasm Gap." *FiveThirtyEight*, FiveThirtyEight, 12 Apr. 2016, https:// fivethirtyeight.com/features/the-gender-orgasm-gap/.

Drewis, Deena. "Portrait of a Girlboss: How Meika Hollender Is Making Sex Healthier for Everyone." November 1, 2016. http://www.girlboss.com/+girlboss/2016/11/1/portrait-of-a-girlboss-how-meika-hollender-ismaking-+sex-healthier-for-everyone.

Ellin, Abby. "For Female-Aphrodisiac Makers, Effort at Parity." *The New York Times.* September 13, 2010. http://www.nytimes.com/2010/09/14/business/media/14adco.html.

Flam, Lisa. "Just Say 'vagina': Using Correct Body Part Names Empowers Kids, Experts Say." TODAY.com. April 23, 2013. https://www.today.com/parents/just-say-vagina-using-correct-body-part-names-empowers-kids-6C9551650.

Griffith, Erin. "Startups Are Failing Because They Make Products No One Wants." *Fortune.com.* March 2, 2015. http://fortune.+com/2014/09/25/why-startups-fail-according-to-their-founders/.

Jezer-Morton, Kathryn. "Two Kids, An IUD, and Then, An Abortion." *Jezebel.* February 18, 2016. http://jezebel.com/two-kids-an-iud-and-then-an-abortion-1758815386.

Laumann, Edward O., A. Paik, and R.C. Rosen. "Sexual Dysfunction in the United States." *JAMA*. February 10, 1999. https://jamanetwork. com/journals/jama/fullarticle/188762.

"Learning: Evaluating an Opportunity." *The Duke Entrepreneurship Manual: A Resource for Entrepreneurs*. Accessed September 24, 2017. https://sites.fuqua.duke.edu/dukeven/new-venture-guidelines/ evaluating-an-opportunity/.

Markets, Research And. "Global Erectile Dysfunction Market 2016-2020 With Bayer, Boston Scientific, Coloplast, Eli Lilly & Pfizer Dominating—Research and Markets." PR Newswire: News Distribution, Targeting and Monitoring. October 12, 2016. http:// www.prnewswire.com/news-releases/global-erectile-dysfunction-market-2016-2020-with-bayer-boston-scientific-coloplast-eli-lilly--pfizer-dominating---research-and-markets-300343543.html.

Militare, Jessica. "2016 College Women of the Year: Suhani Jalota." *Glamour*. April 05, 2017. https://www.glamour.com/story/suhani-jalota-2016-college-women-of-the-year.

Network. Directed by Sidney Lumet. United States: United Artists, 1976. Film.

Newman, Judith. "Sex-Ed for Grown-Ups: A Roundup of Relationship Self-Help." *The New York Times*. April 19, 2017. Accessed August 24, 2017. https://www.nytimes.com/2017/04/19/books/review/help-desk-sex-relationship-self-help.html?mcubz=0.

"Obstetrical and Gynecological Devices; Reclassification of Single-Use Female Condom, To Be Renamed Single-Use Internal Condom." *Federal Register*. December 04, 2017. https://www.federalregister.gov/

documents/2017/12/04/2017-26011/obstetrical-and-gynecological-devices-reclassification-of-single-use-female-condom-to-be-renamed.

Olonisakin, Dami. "According To A US Study, These Are The Two Most Popular Forms Of Sexual Behavior." *IFLScience*. September 18, 2017. http://www.iflscience.com/health-and-medicine/affection-and-romance-most-popular-forms-of-sexual-behavior-says-new-us-study/.

Papisova, Vera. *Teen*, October 7, 2015. https://www.teenvogue.com/story/cancer-chemotherapy-fertility-personal-story.

Peart, Karen N. "The Science of Baby-making Still a Mystery for Many Women." *YaleNews*. January 28, 2014. Accessed August 31, 2017. https://news.yale.edu/2014/01/27/science-baby-making-still-mystery-many-women.

Reinhardt, Andy. "Steve Jobs on Apple's Resurgence." *Business Week*. May 12, 1998. http://allaboutstevejobs.com/sayings/stevejobsinterviews/bw98.php.

Research and Markets. "Erectile Dysfunction Market - Global Outlook and Forecast 2018-2023." *Research and Markets - Market Research Reports - Welcome*. 13 Feb. 2018, http://www.researchandmarkets.com/research/kwz4rc/global_erectile?w=4.Scherl.

Scherl, Rachel Braun. "Words to Live By, Graduates!" *The Huffington Post*. May 20, 2013. Accessed November 03, 2017. https://www.huffingtonpost.com/rachel-braun-scherl/words-to-live-by-graduates_b_3299145.html.

Schmid, Thacher. "The Best Startup Pitch in Town? A Portland-Based Company That Soothes the Symptoms of Menopause." *Willamette Week*. March 24, 2017. http://www.wweek.com/technology/2017/03/24/the-best-startup-pitch-in-town-a-portland-based-company-that-soothes-the-symptoms-of-menopause/.

"Semprae Laboratories." Stanford Graduate School of Business. Accessed June 22, 2017. https://www.gsb.stanford.edu/faculty-research/case-studies/semprae-laboratories.

Stahl, Ashley. "Here's What Burnout Costs You." *Forbes*. April 16, 2016. Accessed September 05, 2017. https://www.forbes.com/sites/ashleystahl/2016/03/04/heres-what-burnout-costs-you/#50221e854e05.

"Suhani Jalota '16 Named 2017 Queen's Young Leader Award Winner." January 30, 2017. https://econ.duke.edu/news/suhani-jalota-16-named-2017-queens-young-leader-award-winner.

"Unintended Pregnancy in the United States." Guttmacher Institute. September 23, 2016. https://www.guttmacher.org/fact-sheet/unintended-pregnancy-united-states.

Van Tassel, Gabrielle. "Sex Education or Sex Ignorance?" *The Huffington Post*. May 03, 2015. Accessed September 24, 2017. http://www.huffingtonpost.com/gabrielle-van-tassel/sex-education-or-sex-igno_b_7199708.html.

Vostral, Sharra L. "Rely and Toxic Shock Syndrome: A Technological Health Crisis." *The Yale Journal of Biology and Medicine*. December 2011. Accessed September 24, 2017. https://www.ncbi.nlm.nih.gov/pubmed/22180682/.

Wertheim, Bonnie. "Options for Periods Include Cups and Special Underwear." *The New York Times*. November 15, 2016. https://www. nytimes.com/2016/11/15/well/live/options-for-periods-include-cups-and-special-underwear.html.